Breaking the Code of Silence

BREAKING THE CODE OF SILENCE

Prominent Leaders Reveal How They Rebound from 7 Critical Mistakes

Dr. Mitchell E. Kusy and Dr. Louellen N. Essex

TAYLOR TRADE PUBLISHING
Dallas • Lanham • Boulder • New York • Toronto • Oxford

Published by Taylor Trade Publishing
An imprint of The Rowman & Littlefield Publishing Group, Inc.
4501 Forbes Boulevard, Suite 200
Lanham, MD 20706

Distributed by National Book Network

Library of Congress Cataloging-in-Publication Data

Kusy, Mitchell.
  Breaking the code of silence : prominent leaders reveal how they rebound from 7 critical mistakes / Mitchell E. Kusy and Louellen N. Essex.— 1st Taylor Trade Pub. ed.
     p. cm.
  Includes bibliographical references and index.
  ISBN 1-58979-118-5 (cloth : alk. paper)
  1. Leadership. I. Essex, Louellen. II. Title.
HD57.7.K87 2004
658.4'092—dc22   2004016403

To Will and Grace

CONTENTS

FOREWORD

Dr. Steve Lundin,
Author of *Fish!* and *Fish! Sticks*

One lesson I have learned well is that every leader must deal with risk. There are risks of action, risks of inaction, and risks that come with simply getting out of bed in the morning. And whenever there is a risk there is a chance of failing.

Leaders don't like the word "failure" and have been creative in their attempts to soften the concept. We talk about flubs, gaffs, hiccups, botches, miscues, trips, muffs, and mess-ups. We have even formed laws with corollaries like "anything that can go wrong will go wrong."

This book is not another attempt to obfuscate risk and failure, but a serious study of how we can rebound from the most frequently occurring mistakes we are likely to make in our leadership lives. There are seven and each has its antidote. I will tell you about the mistakes; you can read on and discover the antidotes.

1. **Engagement Gridlock** is a mistake made by leaders who want everything right and believe that if you want a job done well you

will do it yourself. This mistaken short-term strategy leaves the leaders' talent pools undeveloped and in the background. And when staff are really needed, they are not ready, nor are their heads in the game.

2. **Misaligned Momentum** is decisive movement in the wrong direction. This is a common mistake made by leaders with exceptional intellectual curiosity. If you are prone to falling in love with your own ideas and drifting away from the strategic focus of the organization, you may want to study the tactics for rebounding from misaligned momentum.

3. **Political Misread** is fueled by our common disdain for politics in the organization. When Peter Block wrote the book *Positive Political Skills*, he attempted to put a good spin on an important subject. Because we have such a love-hate relationship with politics, we all need a way to rebound from out political misreads.

4. **Too Much Too Soon** is a mistake waiting to happen for those on the "fast track" and for any leader who pushes the envelope. Any one of us could look up one day and realize we are not fully prepared for the prize assignment we have just landed. What should you do when your dreams are answered and you have too much too soon?

5. **Miscued Decision-Making** focuses on the critical error of making really bad decisions that can often put a whole career at risk. There are no guarantees, but there is a strategy to rebound from them gracefully.

6. **Stifled Communication** describes a situation in which the flow of information is so unpredictable and sparse that the leader is operating without full knowledge of key factors. When communication shuts down, risks increase. How can you open a closed environment and rebuild the flow of information? Stay tuned as you read this book.

7. **Bungled Hiring** is a mistake we all make at least once. Leaders pride themselves in using their intuition and having a "gut feel" for things. At the same time, some interviewees are very good at reading you and telling you what you want to hear. When this mistake is made, it needs to be dealt with quickly; your key to rebounding from bungled hiring can be found in the text.

Breaking the Code of Silence is a research-based and practical book about a very important subject for leaders. It assumes we all make mistakes and presents some great ideas about how we can rebound quickly when that happens to us. Read on and get ready for the unwanted inevitable, or keep it handy for those little surprises that organizational life always has in store for each of us.

MISTAKE RECOVERY
The New Leadership Competency

BREAKING THE CODE OF SILENCE

This is the book that almost didn't get written. In contacting successful leaders to interview them about their own critical mistakes and how they recovered, we received widely mixed reactions—from overwhelming acceptances to gracious declines to no return calls to flat-out no's. Our work as researchers and consultants caused us to question the value of our research when we experienced difficulty finding a population to interview! We were worried about failure being so buried in the closet that leaders might be in a morass of wanting to talk about it, but not knowing if they should. Quite frankly, we even wondered if many leaders acknowledged failure long enough to learn from it. Our fears were confirmed. In our attempts to connect the dots with initial conversations, many of our voice-mail messages, letters, and e-mail correspondence remained unanswered or were responded to with "no thanks." And even though some agreed to an interview, they backed out with reasons ranging from "not a good time" to "I can't add anything of value" to "I'm not the right person" to "I'm not willing to be associated with the topic." Among many leaders, there was a code of silence warning: Do not talk about your mistakes! Fortunately, we were eventually able to identify a group of highly successful leaders who responded with stories from their own experiences. These leaders helped break this code by admitting their mistakes and revealing their recovery strategies. In this book, we share our research on not only the seven types of burning mistakes topflight leaders make, but also how they skillfully rebound from them. The rebound strategy a leader uses is the new leadership competency—it is a *resume-builder*, if you will. It is a leadership hallmark that, when properly executed, can transform a negative situation into a badge of success. In *Breaking the Code of Silence*, we describe seven of the most common, critical mistakes leaders have made and expend the greatest energy not on the mistakes but rather on what we refer to as the "rapid rebound" strategies.

Let's consider an important definition so we're all working off the same page. Our use of the term *critical* emphasizes that these are not ordinary mistakes; they are fierce, inflammatory errors that could have the potential of dashing a leader's career and radically crashing an organization—if an immediate rebound strategy were not put in place. We use the *rebound* metaphor because it takes its root from several contexts, all of which are relevant here. The most obvious is from the sports world. Defensive rebounding is the key to winning at basketball. Picking off the balls that come from your own and others' missed shots requires aggressiveness, positioning, and determination. Rebounders are typically elbowed, shoved, pushed, or even knocked to the floor. Ineffective players lose the opportunity to recover from the missed shot when they stand around watching the flight of the ball, maybe only for a moment, rather than going for the rebound. Successful players strategically recover the ball because they have trained themselves to rapidly assess where the ball is coming off the rim, then apply the right technique to turn the failed attempt into a scored point.

We have discovered that successful leaders have learned the same approaches. With acceptance of their own fallibility and the confidence to recover, they have learned an array of strategies for rebounding from even the most devastating failures. In our own consulting practices, we began putting our fingers on the pulse of this new beat—how successful leaders manage failure. We observed that some unsuccessful leaders derailed their careers by the way they managed mistakes, while others were able to soar ahead and actually strengthen their career trajectory as a result of missing some of their "shots." We've also recognized that the speed with which the leader is able to rebound is critical in these times of rapid change, so what successful leaders do with critical failures involves repositioning their failures and retrieving their careers, acts that must be executed with lightening speed.

Looking back in time we found that the same observation held true for famous leaders with whom you are probably familiar. These successful leaders have failures under their belts. R. H. Macy faltered several times before he emerged successfully with his New York store. Abraham Lincoln was defeated for the legislature in 1832; for U.S. Congress in 1843, 1846, and 1848; and defeated for the U.S. Senate twice in 1855 and 1858—even for the vice presidency in 1856.

THE STRATEGIC PRATFALL EFFECT:
WHAT JFK AND ANN LANDERS HAD IN COMMON

Critical failures, with follow-up rebounds, strengthen a leader's credibility. In what is now known as the strategic-pratfall effect, psychologists have found that people actually identify with leaders who openly admit to their mistakes. Surprised? Consider the fact that President John F. Kennedy's popularity increased dramatically after the mistreatment of the Bay of Pigs offensive—not after his assassination nor after his successful handling of the Cuban Missile Crisis. Why? Because he assumed responsibility for this—demonstrating that he was capable of mistakes and, thus, he was perceived as much more "human." Even more fascinating is that pollsters have assessed the aftermath of this situation as being one of the pinnacles of Kennedy's popularity. Some psychologists have noted that people despise those who are "perfect" and always successful because these characteristics are exactly what we yearn for and don't have.

A more contemporary example demonstrating the power of the strategic-pratfall effect is none other than the late "Ann Landers." While we don't personally have enough data to accurately assess Landers' leadership ability, we do have a scenario demonstrating what the strategic-pratfall effect did for her career. First, some information about Landers' success. She was the most widely syndicated columnist in the world with her column appearing in excess of 1,200 newspapers, accumulating an estimated daily readership of more than 90 million. In a 1975 column, she told readers about her divorce, which some view as catapulting her success even more. This situation made her more approachable, more real, and more believable. Please note that we are not saying that Landers did this as an intentional strategy. What we are saying is that being more human and exposing one's vulnerabilities are certainly assets in recovery management.

MISTAKES AND BEYOND

What makes *Breaking the Code of Silence* so different? We discovered that very little has been written about *specific* strategies leaders use to recover from *specific* types of mistakes. In *Breaking the Code of Silence* you'll see applicable wisdom and step-by-step templates suggesting tailor-made actions for leaders who falter critically. While our examples, observations, and follow-up actions demonstrate that obstacles can be overcome, we do want to be clear that this is *not* a book about organizational mistakes. There are plenty of books on the market dealing with these kinds of failures. This book is different in that it deals with leadership mistakes and provides leaders with a game plan for a *speedy* recovery. We emphasize *speedy* because some books have generated recovery plans that require prolonged self-analysis and reflection. *Breaking the Code of Silence* extends beyond these approaches that advocate that you "pull yourself up by your bootstraps," "get on with your life," and "learn from your failure." These are important and valuable lessons, but what we have ascertained from our interviewed leaders is that these are not enough. Champion leaders take immediate and deliberate actions in response to each kind of critical failure.

Our book also recognizes that not all failure is recoverable. There is a generalized notion that everyone can recover from everything. This is just not so. In *Breaking the Code of Silence*, we'll share the two mistakes from which recovery is just about impossible.

We all learned early on that failure is bad. In school, an F was associated with failure—a poor grade. This connotes nothing but negative images and bad feelings for most people. The fear of failure has caused many people to avoid pursuing risky endeavors, tough paths, or their wildest dreams. Failure is often viewed as an unpleasant end, something we should avoid so we don't experience the angst. Some leaders are so obsessed with the dread of failure that they become almost paralyzed when faced with any type of innovation and ultimately become risk-averse.

Fortunately, there are successful leaders who have come to terms with all the negative "stuff" associated with failure. Each has recognized that their failures were not only manageable, but also necessary ingredients for their success. They have acknowledged the paradox that success requires a willingness to risk failure. By coming to terms with their failures, they were able to realize how these mistakes helped to define who they are today. Follow Gregg Steinhafel's lead here. As president of Target Stores, Gregg models this philosophy and art of mistake recovery as every leader's domain—so much so that he takes ownership of its power. According to Gregg, "Lead the recovery process; don't let it just happen or don't count on others to clean up your mess. Jump in with both feet and demonstrate your willingness to get in there and course correct." Similarly, Terry Gross, host and executive producer of *Fresh Air* on National Public Radio, accentuated this perspective in an interview in *O* magazine (Funderburg 2001): "We're taught to be afraid of failure. But it's really not the worst thing if you're resilient enough to get up and keep going. Sometimes when you fail, it's for a good reason. You're doing the wrong thing."

OUR RESEARCH APPROACHES AND GENERAL FINDINGS

Before writing this book, we did our homework in several ways—all focused on learning more about leadership flops and subsequent rebounds. Our research methodology of 250 structured and unstructured interviews took several twists and turns as we searched hard for leaders who would give us their real stories. We pursued an eight-phase approach to this research.

1. We scoured the relevant literature from 1994 to 2004.

In preparing to write this book, we first reviewed the current leadership literature from the past ten years. Then we extracted the themes of what other researchers and authors had found.

To further hone in our research, we defined two core concepts—"success" and "leadership." We defined success as achieving something of worth for which there is documented evidence within the organization. We accept leadership guru John Kotter's definition of leadership as the "process of moving a group (or groups) of people in some direction through (mostly) non-coercive means" (Kotter 1988, 16). A leader is anyone who engages in this as defined by Kotter.

Our review also strongly suggested that making mistakes, learning from the experience, and moving on is a critical cycle for promoting individual and organizational risk-taking. We discovered the increasing importance of taking risks and learning from failure as the speed of change and innovation has accelerated. But we found little to guide leaders in knowing exactly what to do (beyond learning from the mistake) when failure knocks on their doors.

2. We learned from hundreds of our own clients and seminar participants.

Over a five-year period from 1999 to 2004, we learned about mistake recovery through informal conversations and interviews with our clients. In working with them, we began to get a clearer picture of critical mistakes and concomitant recovery strategies. They taught us that not all leaders learn from their mistakes nor do all leaders recover from their failures. It's not enough to take risks and fall on your face. We learned that the secret to capitalizing on the failure appeared to be in applying the *right* strategy *immediately* following a *specific* situation. *Right* because the strategy had to be tailor-made for the situation at hand. *Immediately* because it had to be swiftly applied. *Specific* because it had to detail the steps necessary to make a good recovery.

3. We developed our research questions.

Both our literature review and work with our clients positioned us to hone in on our three core research questions:

   a. What are the critical mistakes successful leaders have made that could have derailed, or actually derailed, their careers and negatively impacted their organizations?
   b. Did they recover?
   c. If so, how?

While we had included many more structured questions as part of our interview process, each question could be classified in one of these broad categories.

4. We conducted interviews with forty successful leaders.

To prepare for our structured interviews using these three questions as a backdrop, we began identifying a population of successful leaders through our professional contacts, consulting practices, and those identified through our literature review. To really hone in on what is a successful leader, we define the successful leader as anyone referenced in an article (e.g., journal, magazine, newspaper) within the past five years or anyone referenced in a conversation with the authors within the past year as being a success (as defined on page 7) *and* referred to at least two times with any of the following terms:

- "Successful"
- "Effective"
- "One of the Best 25 Managers in the World" (*Business Week,* January 2001)
- "Small Business Person of the Year" (*U.S. Small Business Administration's List,* 1999)

We validated our findings from our initial list of leaders by formally interviewing another forty individuals, ages twenty-five to seventy-four years, from a variety of organizations: small, medium, and large in size; profit and nonprofit. The leaders we selected were those with outstanding successes. Some of the leaders we interviewed include vice presidents, presidents, CEOs, team leaders, directors, supervisors, and managers; a U.S. senator and a cabinet member of a U.S. president; business partners and owners.

5. We also conducted structured interviews with twenty leadership coaches.

We chose twenty leadership coaches whose titles included executive coach, outplacement consultant, or recruiter and were either in independent practice or worked for a consulting organization. A leadership consultant was a professional whose primary occupation was to facilitate successes of leaders through insight, counseling, and feedback. Many of those we interviewed suggested other successful leaders whom we added to our list of interviewees.

6. We analyzed the interview data.

We carefully analyzed the interview data and identified seven critical failures and the corresponding rebound strategies. We then determined that we needed richer, more robust data to really zero in on the recovery strategies—more so than the initial set of questions provided.

7. We conducted an additional twenty-five structured interviews with case scenarios.

We developed a new interview format designed to enrich the findings we had already gathered. We added scenarios depicting critical leadership mistakes that respondents had described during our first round of interviews. We validated these scenarios through expert opinion and then asked twenty-five successful leaders to study the scenarios and tell us how they would respond to the scenarios presented.

Using the revised scenarios, we assigned two of them to each leader interviewed. For this round, we chose leaders from two contexts:

a. High profile, successful leaders who were experienced and publicly known, or

b. Those leaders who have been hailed as benchmarks of success as defined previously on page 7.

8. We analyzed the additional interview and scenario data.

One general finding that surprised us was that the high-profile leaders we had interviewed were even more candid about their personal mistakes than less high-profile leaders. They provided more detailed information than less well-known leaders. How do we interpret this statistic? First, our interpretation is that these leaders have had to practice their rebound strategies more often because they are under the harshest scrutiny from the public—both those within the organization who look to them as models and those outside who are key stakeholders in their success (and failure). Second, everything is out in the open with these leaders anyway, so it's harder for them to hide their mistakes than for other leaders.

There was one slight turn of events with these high-profile leaders that, quite frankly, caught us by surprise. While they were more candid than others, they did not readily step to the plate when we requested interviews with them. In fact, our acceptance rate from these higher-profile leaders was about 25 percent, while the acceptance rate was approximately 75 percent for lower-profile leaders from the initial round of forty interviews, as figure intro.1 illustrates. How do we juggle this statistic, which seems paradoxical from the previously mentioned finding that high-profile leaders were more candid about their mistakes? We believe that our high-profile leaders were more concerned about their public image. And because their mistakes were quite public, they had been forced to either openly address the mistake or dodge it by not talking about it. Our high-profile leaders did just that—almost in an absolute way. They either refused our interview or talked so openly about it that we were simply awed by their candor and resiliency.

We thought that perhaps the leaders who rejected our interviews were not as successful as the ones who accepted. Please note that this is speculation on our part and we don't have hard data to back up this interpolation with the exception of the studies from the Center for Creative Leadership in Greensboro, North Carolina. The research of this highly respected leadership development firm that attracts client leaders from all over the world demonstrates that successful leaders report more mistakes than unsuccessful leaders.

Throughout the rest of this book, we will present the analyzed data on the actual mistakes and the immediate recovery strategies that were most effective for these successful leaders.

FIGURE I.1.

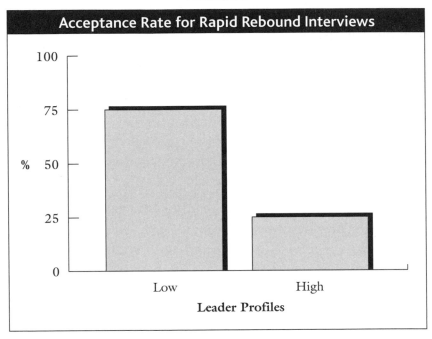

Acceptance Rate for Rapid Rebound Interviews

OUR RESULTS DEBUNK SIX PREVALENT MYTHS

Our findings clearly debunk some of the myths commonly associated with leadership failure, as summarized in box intro.1.

MYTH 1: Low-profile leaders are more likely to admit their mistakes.

In the *Fortune* cover story, "So You Fail . . . Now Bounce Back!" (Sellers 1995), the leaders who are featured are prominent executives: marketing executive Sergio Zyman of New Coke "fame," Steven Jobs and John Sculley from Apple Computer and their initial failed attempt to compete with IBM in the business environment, and American Express executive Anne Busquet whose Optima

---

BOX I.1.

6 Myths about Leadership Recovery

MYTH 1: Low-profile leaders are more likely to admit their mistakes.

MYTH 2: Learning from failure alone poises one to succeed.

MYTH 3: All mistakes are recoverable.

MYTH 4: Don't wear mistakes on your shirtsleeves.

MYTH 5: Mistake recovery is generic.

MYTH 6: Admitting your personality flaws is a good recovery mechanism.

Card unit bombed. Many of our interviewees (executives and non-executives alike) described how admitting a mistake, applying the right strategy, and quickly moving forward were critical competencies for advancing their careers. These high-profile leaders, then, explode the myth that mistake identification is only for low-profile leaders.

It may appear in figure intro.1 that it may be true that low-profile leaders are more likely to admit their mistakes than high-profile leaders since the low-profile interview acceptance rate was 75 percent and the high-profile interview acceptance rate was 25 percent. However, when we examined what leaders said during the interviews, the high-profile leaders were much more candid and revealing about their mistakes.

MYTH 2: Learning from failure is enough to succeed.

While we have suggested failures may be necessary to build optimum leadership competency, it's not only the learning that makes a difference. It is how skillfully the recovery strategy was executed *and* how quickly. The most recent myth, à la the dot-com frenzy, is that a string of dot-com failures is a benchmark to ultimate success. Well, maybe. We say "maybe" because this is predicated by a big "if"— *if* the leader fails "properly." This sentiment is echoed by Efrem Dryer, president of CEE Inc., who shares the importance of mistakes he has made: "If I had not flunked out of college, I would not have started my business. If I had not hired an employee that eventually cost me thousands of dollars, I would not have implemented more in-depth hiring procedures . . . but when you fail and do so properly, you learn, not fail." And according to Kamran Elahian (Pham 2000), who has started ten companies in the Silicon Valley since 1981, "True success is management of failure" (D9). We discovered that by failing "properly," leaders decipher a pattern from their string of failures and design a subsequent action plan. While learning will probably help someone manage future failures, it's not what will help the leader handle critical mistakes being made at the moment.

MYTH 3: All mistakes are recoverable.

While personal recovery from the anguish of a mistake is always possible, the leader's ability to recover within a given organization is not always possible. Some mistakes are fatal errors and will derail a career path with lightning speed.

In our own research, we uncovered two specific types of errors that fell into this category. The first is aberrations of trust that compromise leader integrity. If people lose trust in you, you might find it easier to hang up your hat. Period. There are many reasons people lose trust in their leaders, but the most pronounced is the situation where ethics—either the leader's own or the ethics of the organization—are compromised. One leadership coach we interviewed is David Bachrach, president of the Physician Executive's Coach. David has spent thirty years in academic medicine, both as an administrative leader and, for the past five years, as a leadership coach to physician executives. David calls these crises in confidence "career killers." Some examples that lead to crises in confidence include the theft of assets, reconfiguration of data, or the stonewalling of important information that others have a right or need to know. According to David and other interviewees, you simply "do not steal or cook up data."

If you look at this situation historically, recovery was difficult for former President Lyndon Johnson. "A leader cannot break trust. It's a disastrous decision in any institution. . . . In his speeches Johnson kept promising that there was light at the end of the tunnel [regarding the Vietnam war]—a promise that proved fatal when he was unable to keep his word . . . leading eventually to Johnson's withdrawal from the presidential race. His retirement was almost unbearable to him, knowing that he failed at the moment his triumph had almost been achieved" (Goodwin 1998, 24). According to Goodwin, "Trust, once broken, is seldom restored." (27).

Consider more recent critical mistakes. Our research would predict that it would be very difficult to restore the legitimacy of selected leaders at such organizations as Enron, Arthur Andersen, the Catholic Church, and WorldCom because of the breach of trust that compromised leader integrity in these organizations. Picture this: leaders apologizing for their lapse of ethical standards or inability to manage the store. Our research would presuppose that this apology would not even begin to reinstate leadership trust because of the horrible losses experienced by others. In this situation, a breach of ethics is unrecoverable on the part of the leader.

The second irretrievable error we discovered in our interviews was associated with mistakes that are foolish. These are errors made on fundamental leadership tasks and indicating gross incompetence. After repeated attempts by others to provide feedback and help them gain self-awareness, some leaders remain change-resistant. One coach we interviewed was Bruce Roselle, Ph.D., president of Roselle Leadership Strategies, Inc. Bruce noted this regarding incompetent leaders: "It's not that they don't change, but rather they don't change enough. . . . They improve from awful to mediocre." This is basically a nonrebound act. So, *all* failure *cannot* be resurrected, as some writers and consultants have thought. Box intro.2 summarizes these two types of nonrecoverable mistakes.

MYTH 4: Don't wear mistakes on your shirtsleeves.

Consider tire maker Bridgestone/Firestone. If you'll recall, Firestone (a subsidiary of Bridgestone and now referred to as "Bridgestone/ Firestone") had to recall over 6.5 million radial auto tires following 119 deaths as a result of tire tread separation, primarily on Ford Explorers. Fortunately, after an extended period of time, Firestone/ Bridgestone acknowledged that it should have been more diligent in monitoring the situation. This is the good news because their specific rebound strategy was that they admitted their mistake in a very public forum. From our perspective, there was a powerful opportunity

---

BOX I.2.

Two Nonrecoverable Mistakes

1. Aberrations of trust that compromise leader integrity.
2. A pattern of foolish mistakes that indicates gross incompetence.

here for leaders at Bridgestone/Firestone to coach others in the organization about what they learned from their mistake. What we advocate is that it is not enough to just admit blame and learn from it yourself—you've got to share this learning with others.

MYTH 5: Mistake recovery is generic.

Some perceive that the same recovery strategy is useful in all situations. Not so. In our research, we have discovered that the types of mistakes made create the need for certain kinds of rebound strategies. Think about it this way. Would you use the same rewards to manage the performance of each of your staff? We hope not. Individuals are motivated by different reinforcers. Then why should one recovery strategy work in all situations? It won't. Why? Because as Gregg Steinhafel, president of Target Stores, noted to us, "Some leaders become overly dependent on one particular leadership style and that simply won't work." In this book, we'll help you understand the critical links between certain kinds of core mistakes and the rebound strategies needed—and how to get out of the quagmire of your own preferred leadership style backfiring.

MYTH 6: Admitting your personality flaws is a good recovery mechanism.

Well, not quite. Some believe that sharing a personality flaw (e.g., shyness) is a great way to rebound from a critical mistake. Our book takes a much more behavioral approach. Leaders we interviewed never identified the admission of personality flaws as key; rather, they acknowledged how their own *behaviors* (e.g., not being assertive enough in asking probing questions versus being shy) contributed to the mistake. This is important here because it is much easier to change behavior than personality. You can do something about your own behavior.

SEVEN CRITICAL MISTAKES AND
REBOUND STRATEGIES DISCOVERED

Along with debunking some popular misconceptions about failing, our results uncovered seven critical mistakes that are immediately recoverable with the right actions. Box intro.3 lists these seven critical mistakes.

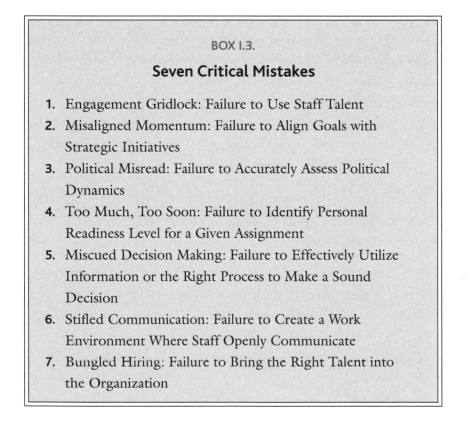

BOX I.3.

Seven Critical Mistakes

1. Engagement Gridlock: Failure to Use Staff Talent
2. Misaligned Momentum: Failure to Align Goals with Strategic Initiatives
3. Political Misread: Failure to Accurately Assess Political Dynamics
4. Too Much, Too Soon: Failure to Identify Personal Readiness Level for a Given Assignment
5. Miscued Decision Making: Failure to Effectively Utilize Information or the Right Process to Make a Sound Decision
6. Stifled Communication: Failure to Create a Work Environment Where Staff Openly Communicate
7. Bungled Hiring: Failure to Bring the Right Talent into the Organization

We have structured this book around these seven critical mistakes and the corresponding rapid rebound strategies. At the start of each chapter, you'll see a fictitious scenario that we created based on our data about a critical leadership mistake. Following this scenario, we offer interpretations from the selected list of leaders and leadership coaches we interviewed, along with our own interpretations. Following each critical error, we provide specific, actionable strategies leaders can use to get out of each type of jam and move back on course. At the end of this book, we provide the background behind the two fatal errors from which a comeback is rare, if not impossible.

Use this book as your guide as you learn the art of strategically responding to mistakes both you and others encounter on the path to optimum leadership.

CHAPTER

ENGAGEMENT GRIDLOCK
Rebound with Rapid Reinvesting

WHAT THE MISTAKE LOOKS LIKE

Samantha O. has aggressively worked her way up the organizational ladder to the position of commissioner of revenue within state government. She is known for her competence, independence, and no-nonsense approach to driving financial reform. Samantha has worked hard and has low tolerance for staff who appear "lazy" or low performing. She expects perfection in herself as well as others.

In assuming her role as commissioner two years ago, Samantha was cautious about delegating important work to her staff. She maintained tight control of major decision making, fearful of what might go wrong if she let staff members whose work she couldn't trust have too much authority. As a result, Samantha has alienated her immediate team and caused her entire organization to become sluggish, since very little can be done without Samantha's direct approval. Everyone feels as if they are walking on eggshells. Staff creativity is stifled, and recently there was an exodus of some of the most talented staff members. Samantha has heard that others intend to follow suit. Morale, exhibited by a lack of commitment to the organization, is at an all-time low since they have concluded they do not have a voice and their ideas are of no interest to Samantha. While some staff have attempted to talk with her about their discontent, Samantha—true to form—has not been listening.

The human resource department recently compiled some exit interview information with Samantha's staff who had left. Clearly, Samantha's disengaging leadership approach was the main reason they gave for resigning. Samantha now realizes she made a huge mistake in her approach to her current role. She stymied staff development and treated them as if they had nothing to offer. While she calls her immediate reports her "team," Samantha knows she has not created a true team atmosphere. She worries now that her own success is highly jeopardized.

THE CAUSES OF ENGAGEMENT GRIDLOCK

Samantha is correct. Her leadership role is at risk in that she has alienated talented staff who now view her as an obstacle to their career development and satisfaction. She has made a major mistake in adopting a leadership style that is stifling rather than enabling. This mistake type we call *engagement gridlock—failure to use staff talent.* From our own research and consulting practices we have found something fascinating about leaders who demonstrate this mistake. They often lack style flexibility—an inability to adjust their sails to varying currents that pass their way. When push comes to shove their default style is solo management. They end up not using the talent at hand, even when it's in their best interests to do so, and subsequently disengage staff.

Leaders most likely to make this mistake are those who have set high standards for themselves and worked relentlessly to achieve their goals. They are independent by nature and tend to be most comfortable working on their own. Delegation poses a tremendous dilemma for leaders prone to making this mistake. While they may acknowledge the importance of giving assignments to others, they are reluctant to do so because they believe no one can perform as well as they can. And when they *do* give assignments to others, these projects seem to require little creativity and lack challenge in that they have little "stretch" capability. These types of leaders fear the outcome will not meet the demanding standards they have set for themselves. Hence, the "delegated" assignments are those where the leader can be sure of the outcome, with little innovation needed.

Our discovery of this mistake type is reinforced by psychologists who deal with issues related to perfectionism. While psychologists have identified several types of perfectionism (Blatt 1995), the one we have noted here is associated with a leader demanding that others achieve unrealistic and exaggerated goals. And because leaders suffering from this form of perfectionism believe that no one can meet their standards, they do it all themselves. The result? Little empowerment of talented individuals *and* ultimately, if this continues unabated, a leader's downfall. For the most severe example of this, let us refresh your memory of Vince Foster, deputy counsel to President Clinton. In an article that appeared in the *Washington Post* (1993), he is seen as an incredibly gifted leader who demanded the most of himself *and* others. He would personally go through twenty drafts if he thought it necessary. He delivered a commencement speech to the University of Arkansas Law School, in which he said,

"Treat every pleading, every brief, every contract, every letter, every daily task as if your career will be judged on it. . . . I cannot make this point to you too strongly." In an ironic turn of events, some say he committed suicide because he felt a personal sense of responsibility for issues in the Clinton administration dealing with White House travel and issues related to the Little Rock Country Club. When any leader takes on such intense, personal responsibilities that should be others', we see the disasters that can occur with engagement gridlock. We are *not* saying that this was definitively associated with his suicide. What we *are* saying is that leaders enter the danger zone of engagement gridlock by not using staff to their utmost potential.

Consider another example: the former CEO of Ford, Jacques Nasser. Intelligent and imaginative, Nasser had a hard time involving others, according to many sources (Healey 2001). Set up as a monarch, Nasser tried to do it all himself rather than coach others to get the job done. And we're talking about an *executive* group he managed! His style of wanting to be something to everyone was his downfall. Plain and simple, others had a difficult time doing anything of significance without the imprimatur of his John Hancock.

We think you'll recognize this type of individual in others *and* maybe in yourself. This behavior runs rampant in organizations, which is the reason we placed it first in our litany of seven critical mistakes. Interestingly, we have found that bulldozers sometimes get their just due. Left unattended, engagement gridlock can cause many staff to bail out, leaving leaders to fend for themselves. In our own consulting practices we have learned that this is often the precursor to the leaders going down as well. One leader of a Fortune 500 financial services organization with which we worked found herself in this very quandary. Her bulldozer style led to a mass exit of quite competent staff. She just didn't get it and refused to react with a recovery plan until it was too late—she was fired. Fascinating to us, she never did understand her role in all of this. The bottom line here is that every leader needs to observe staff bailouts as sometimes setting the stage for his or her own demise. So that this doesn't happen to you, box 1.1 lists leader behaviors that typically result in engagement gridlock. Using this template to help you assess your own vulnerable spots is the first step in a successful rebound.

REBOUND WITH RAPID REINVESTING

If not tuned in to the hazards of engagement gridlock, leaders may be left in the dust without the needed horsepower to maneuver the work of the department. In the most negative of cases, staff respond to engagement gridlock by leaving. Fast action is crucial to this rebound strategy in order to stop the exodus of talented staff. This is precisely what T. J. Rodgers, founder and president of Cypress Semiconductor Corporation, initiated in his own organization. He has been called one of the most fiercely competitive leaders in Silicon Valley. Several years

---

BOX 1.1.

Behaviors That Result in Engagement Gridlock

- Perfectionism to a fault
- Lack of understanding of your staff's needs
- Unwillingness to delegate interesting or important work
- Noninclusion of staff in critical decision making or problem solving
- Nondevelopment of staff talent
- Inadequate feedback to staff regarding *how* decisions will be made

ago, after intervening in a situation where two valued executives were ready to join other companies, Rodgers drafted a memo, "What to Do When a Valued Employee Quits" (Kirsner 1998). This subsequently became the company's blueprint for successfully retaining valued staff who had announced their intent to leave, and in some cases had already secured new jobs. He emphasizes that fast action in this critical situation means responding "within five minutes" of discovering your valued staff are heading out the door.

We have discovered that fast action must be coupled with the briefest of communication that has the power to persuade. For a closer look at this, consider our introductory scenario, which presented Samantha's engagement gridlock. We asked a sample of our interviewees to examine Samantha's predicament and give us advice on what they would do, or have done, in a similar situation. Nearly all suggested Samantha's only hope for recovery lies in her ability to act quickly to gather feedback about her approach, then reinvest in staff by creating new lines of communication and empowerment to retain what staff remains. At the same time, she must reverse the outflow of talent. This requires a three-part strategy. When encountering this problem, here are the rapid rebound strategies that will allow you to get back on track and effectively recover:

1. Immediately clear your calendar.

Once you become aware that staff members are leaving because of your engagement gridlock style, while those who remain are filled with anger and frustration, cancel the next activity on your schedule and refocus your priorities. Cypress Semiconductor's Rodgers says, "Any delay [even saying "I'll talk to you after our staff meeting"] is unacceptable" (Kirsner 1998). Nothing is more important at this point than taking action to prevent further disaster.

2. Listen intensely, separating your feelings from the facts.

Face your detractors directly by asking questions (box 1.2) designed to reassure staff—best held through one-on-one meetings. If you believe there is not a chance your staff will speak honestly with you, utilize a trusted third party who might be a member of the human resource department's staff, an outside consultant, or leadership coach. If you have a mentor or close colleague who has observed your leadership approach, ask this individual for candid feedback as well.

In Samantha's case she should begin her exploration by reviewing with a human resources professional the exit interview data of the ex-staff she most admires and would rehire if she could. Then she should have conversations with the current staff she most values. The leadership coaches we interviewed were adamant that successful leaders were able to hear critical feedback and learn from it as part of a reflective process. Warren Bennis and Burt Nanus in their work *Leaders: Strategies for Taking Charge* (1997) discussed the differences between failing and learning. The leaders they studied, in fact, rejected the use of the word "failure" and used synonyms like

---

BOX 1.2.

Diagnostic Questions to Ask Gridlocked Staff

1. What parts of your work in our unit most effectively use your talents?
2. What specific things get in the way of you utilizing your talents?
3. In order for you to believe your talents are being utilized, what would *I* have to do differently?

"mistake," "glitch," and "bungle." Their attitude about criticism centered on the learning opportunities it provided, fusing positive self-regard with optimism. Effective leaders, Bennis and Nanus demonstrated, have the confidence to know they can turn the mistake into learning, then move forward. In *13 Fatal Errors Managers Make and How You Can Avoid Them* (1985), W. Steven Brown describes the failure formula: "People fail in direct proportion to their willingness to accept socially acceptable excuses for failure." Managers who fail blame others. Managers who rebound successfully take full responsibility for their role in the situation.

3. Fight hard to regain staff confidence.

Once you've heard the feedback, wage battle on two fronts: with those staff you've just barely managed to retain and with those who are poised to resign. Carefully prepare your response to the feedback you've received, making sure it includes the following components:

a. A *thank you* to staff for their feedback.
b. A *summary of the feedback* you've heard in language that is behaviorally specific and concrete.
c. An *acknowledgment of inadequately using staff talent*. Then give two or three specific examples that demonstrate you understand how you could have acted differently. Don't cloud your message with excuses; this will reverse the message you want to give.
d. A *description of new behaviors* you intend to adopt.

To regain staff confidence, these are the four critical steps. Don't overlook any of these. Begin with thanking staff for their feedback. Second, respond with what you have heard in a brief, summary format, and check it out with others to make sure you have heard it the way it was intended.

Third, acknowledge the inappropriate use (or nonuse) of staff talent. This acknowledgment should include some strong empathy on your part and should demonstrate that you are now placing yourself in their shoes—and don't like what you see related to your own engagement gridlock behaviors. Before you trash the idea that empathy is too soft and "touchy-feely," consider the research of Daniel Goleman of *Emotional Intelligence* (1995) fame. In his research, Goleman discovered that empathy plays a critical role in talent retention (Goleman 1998). Empathy is now more important than ever because, in this era of tremendous knowledge management, good staff who leave are likely to do so with critical company knowledge. Empathy at this stage of the game will help you keep good talent where it belongs—in your organization.

In the fourth phase, as you describe your new approach, let staff know exactly what behaviors you will endeavor to do less often and those you intend to replace with alternative behaviors. Be cautious at this stage—don't overcommit *and* don't overexpose. To our first point of not overcommitting, we suggest you consider the movie *What About Bob?* where actor Richard Dreyfuss played a psychiatrist advocating "baby steps" for his clients pursuing behavioral change. In the film, Dreyfuss is henpecked by patient Bob who just won't leave him alone—even when the good doctor is on vacation. Bob follows him everywhere and can't do anything without him. Dreyfuss's famous "baby steps" is also aligned with how we coach leaders at these crossroads, whereby they are to choose those positive alternative behaviors that will give them the highest impact and be relatively easy to accomplish. Be realistic here. Consider the research on unfulfilled promises. Norcross, Ratzin, and Payne (1989) did research on New Year's resolutions and found that people make the same resolutions year after year and vow on average to stop a particular vice ten times! Almost 25 percent of resolvers give up by the end of the first week; 40 percent stop after six months. Researchers call this the *false hope syndrome* (Polivy and Herman 1999, 2000). This phenomenon incorporates first, undertaking a difficult or impossible task; second, people convincing themselves that with just a few "adjustments" success is within easy reach; and third, after more attempts and failure, those people limiting their expectations for the future. By taking appropriate "baby steps," leaders will reduce the probability that the false hope syndrome will occur for themselves and their staff.

To our second point of the danger of overexposing yourself, we recommend that leaders *not* acknowledge those deficits that can be seen as flaws impossible to correct. This will put you in a worse situation than you're already in. For example, one of our clients, a vice president at an international university, did not involve highly competent staff in important decisions that affected them. After repeated attempts at this, they were ticked off and ready to walk. This VP thought he could regain their confidence by telling them that his personality is one of a rugged individualist. In this case, people perceived that being an individualist was in his nature. To regain staff confidence, this leader decided to seek consensus in more of his decisions—and invited feedback as to how he was doing on this from others. This worked like a charm. He would still be an individualist, but with a creative twist of seeking consensus as appropriate.

As you can see, we're advocating for keeping the mistake in perspective here when it isn't a fatal flaw. This is precisely what Princess Diana did when she made public her eating disorder. She exposed a serious flaw (but one that was correctable). Subsequently, she was seen in a better light—an outcome of a leader who recovers successfully at this stage. Our rule is to never reveal a weakness that a leader can't do something about. If this is the case, the leader needs to remain silent.

Sometimes, you may not know precisely what to do differently. Here, it may take a credible individual holding up a mirror, showing you the errors of your ways in a critical and objective manner. Do this with someone you trust—a leadership coach, a colleague, or someone from within the human resources department in your organization. While we have discovered this in our own research, don't just take our word for it. In hosts of research studies, coaching comes out on top as *the* strategy for building such behaviors as empathy, listening, and motivating others—all critical components for immediate recovery of disengaged staff. Why is leadership coaching so helpful here for leaders who can't pinpoint alternative behaviors to regain staff confidence? According to the most recent brain research, these behaviors emanate from the neurotransmitters of the limbic system within our brains. Learning through the limbic system is best facilitated through feedback and practice—prime work of leadership coaches. And when a leader cannot engage in this, simple observation of good role models and practice is a next-best alternative.

Finding a mentor is exactly what Mike Espy did. For those not familiar with this name, Mike was the U.S. secretary of agriculture in President Clinton's administration. After allegations that he was involved with accepting gifts that indicated a conflict of interest, he resigned. While he was exonerated several years later, his mentor helped him design a reconstruction plan. While Mike's critical error was not one of engagement gridlock of staff, mentoring and coaching may work in a number of cases. However, one of the scenarios we have found coaching and mentoring to be the most successful with is the engagement gridlock problem.

When developing a description of what you are going to do differently, consider a continuum of decision-making styles that clearly define what method you will use in each of four contexts. In *Fast Forward Leadership* (Essex and Kusy 1999), we described the following guidelines for using each style on a continuum from no input from others to their complete involvement, as box 1.3 summarizes.

Leader decides, zero input. The leader makes a decision without input from others. In our work, we have discovered the best situations for applying this style include times of crisis, when the individual/team does not have the requisite skills to contribute to the decision, or when the individual or team may not care about the decision or be affected by it. Leaders must do a diligent job of explaining *why* they are making the decision primarily alone and the forms of support they will need from those who will implement it.

Leader decides with input. The decision is clearly the leader's here, but the leader directly solicits feedback and has a responsibility to inform others how it was utilized to make the decision. Set the ground rules up front: you want the input, will consider it, but may not use all of it. Then complete the loop; report back on what input you did

---

BOX 1.3.

Decision-Making Continuum

1. Leader decides, zero input.
2. Leader decides with input.
3. Leader and others decide together with consensus.
4. Others decide; the leader may or may not be involved.

use and how, as well as why, you rejected some of what you heard. If you really have no intention of reflecting on the input, then go back to the first phase on the continuum (leader decides, zero input). Messages that do not match your actions do more harm than good.

Leader and others decide together with consensus. Using this approach, the leader becomes part of the decision-making group. Here, your voice is simply one of many; the rule of decision making is consensus—discussing until a group mind-set is reached on the issue. We recommend voting only as a last resort because voting has a tendency to polarize a group into "winners" and "losers." One of the pitfalls we have seen of the consensus process is that it can eat up valuable time. The approach we recommend to expedite this process is to provide the team with parameters (e.g., here's the amount of time we can spend on consensus; if the decision isn't reached by a certain time, here's how the decision will be made).

Others decide; the leader may or may not be involved. When using this decision-making approach, the leader literally gets out of the way, allowing others to make decisions independently. The leader serves as a resource for the individual or group, on call as needed. The leader still needs to set the goal, provide parameters, and even redirect if needed. The leader's role is to delegate and get out of way, but not disappear. This individual must be available to coach, give feedback, and troubleshoot.

For those staff already on their way out the door, begin a parallel recovery strategy. Meet with them individually, focusing on convincing them to stay. Your goal here is to win them over. Rodgers, when describing his success with the Cypress talent recovery blueprint, says that the employee must be convinced that quitting is a big mistake and that you will single-handedly work to rectify your part of the problem (Kirsner 1998). Often this requires bringing in executives to help add weight to your case. In preparation for this part of the strategy, it will be critical for you to garner the support of other leaders who can influence those ready to bolt from your organization. This will require reviewing with them the issues you have uncovered as well as your plan to rectify the situation, making a hard sell that you are committed to change.

In both cases, your goal should be to emphasize your commitment to change and the decision-making/delegation model you have redesigned. Be specific in what you delineate and give those you are attempting to influence your commitment to make their work life more satisfying. Table 1.1 provides a template and

TABLE 1.1.

Script Template for Regaining Staff Confidence	
What you do:	**What you say:**
1. Discuss with the team a summary of the feedback you have heard.	"As you know, I have been asking you about my leadership style as it relates to how effectively I use your skills and abilities. I have learned some very valuable things from each of you. This is what I have heard. I'd like to check it out with you, and I welcome your feedback. I've learned that many of you feel I make decisions without your input, yet the outcome of those decisions significantly affects you. I've also learned that there are tasks I do that many of you would like to have the opportunity to be involved in. For example . . . "

What you do:	What you say:
2. Acknowledge and thank staff.	"Thank you for being candid about what I need to do to improve.
3. Outline your specific plan of new behaviors you intend to adopt.	"I am committed to making significant changes so that your work life will be more satisfying. I want this to be a great place to work for all of us. I will outline specifically some new behaviors I will be pursuing to successfully engage your creative talents. To delegate more effectively, I will:

- Talk with each of you about your capabilities and proficiencies needing further development.
- Delegate responsibilities when you have those capabilities.
- Work with you in determining your skills and motivation to improve a specific proficiency needing further development.
- Determine what needs to be done to specifically enhance this proficiency."

"I commit to delegating more successfully. To do this, I will also need periodic feedback from you as to how well I'm doing. It may take a while for you to trust this process, but I do hope my behavior demonstrates I am true to my word."

"Thank you again for your suggestions and the opportunity to work with you on this."

mock script for using talent more successfully by regaining staff confidence.

Leaders who effectively solve the engagement gridlock problem have a tendency to see failure as an opportunity. This is one of Donald Winkler's (chairman and CEO of Ford Motor Credit Co.) ten principles: "Be willing to see failure as a stepping-stone to success" (Hammonds 2000). We believe that leaders who do nothing about engagement gridlock have missed an opportunity to let their true colors shine through.

Box 1.4 summarizes the steps that any leader should take if enmeshed in engagement gridlock.

PROACTIVE HINDSIGHT

Now that you understand the mistake and the rebound strategies, you have a road map for what to do immediately following this mistake should you make it. In addition to the immediate recovery strategies, at the end of each chapter we will provide a Proactive Hindsight section to help you should you have a tendency to make these mistakes often. Here, you will see selected strategies you can use to avoid making them in the future (table 1.2).

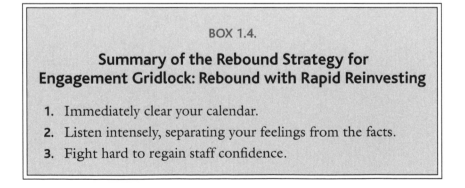

BOX 1.4.

Summary of the Rebound Strategy for Engagement Gridlock: Rebound with Rapid Reinvesting

1. Immediately clear your calendar.
2. Listen intensely, separating your feelings from the facts.
3. Fight hard to regain staff confidence.

In the first of the gridlock behaviors—lack of understanding your staff's needs and wants—it's important to make a continuous effort as a proactive strategy. By this we mean that the leader is continually assessing project satisfaction and importance. At times, we find leaders do one or the other, and then find themselves in a morass. Even when a project is not personally satisfying, if the leader can stress how critical this project is to organizational success, there is less of a probability that engagement gridlock will occur.

The second gridlock behavior—not delegating interesting or important work—means the leader must assess ability and motivation. Ability focuses on a skills orientation. Do they have the skills to do the job? Motivation is not as intuitive as many leaders believe. To assess motivation, we suggest looking at such variables as whether they want to do the project, have the requisite confidence, and have potential reinforcers—either tangible or intangible.

Leaders need to use this model as well for the third of the gridlock behaviors—not including staff in decision making or problem solving. The reason? We have discovered, in this scenario, that leaders are often fearful that staff may not know enough about a certain area (ability) or may not care about the decision (motivation).

Fourth, to proactively maneuver around the nondevelopment of staff talent, leaders must focus their efforts on what will create the most organizational value and be the easiest to implement (usually because someone has motivation to do this). Developing talent in areas where there is little internal interest is futile.

The fifth area—not letting staff know how decisions will be made—is the simplest to correct but the most devastating if it's not. Why? Because if there is a disconnect between what a leaders says (e.g., "I want your input") and what the leader does (e.g., acts without the input), trust will erode. And we know from the research of leadership guru Warren Bennis that the main determinant of trust is reliability—do the leaders do what they say they will do?

Use this template as a backdrop for making yourself more gridlock-averse. Although you have a running board of the rebound strategies to use at a moment's notice, you'll be a more successful leader if you avoid this error in the first place.

TABLE 1.2.

Engagement Gridlock Behavior and What a Leader Needs to Do to Decrease the Probability of Future Reoccurrence	
Engagement Gridlock Behaviors	**Proactive Engagement**
1. Lack of understanding of your staff's needs and wants	Periodically, make a concerted effort to ask staff what types of projects are most satisfying to them *and* most critical to the organization.
2. Not delegating interesting or important work	If they have the ability and motivation, delegate these satisfying, critical responsibilities to them.
3. Not including staff in decision making or problem solving	Include staff in decisions *if* they have both the ability and motivation to be involved.
4. Not developing staff talent	Initiate your staff development around those skills that are both most critical to the organization *and* easiest to implement.

Engagement Gridlock Behaviors	Proactive Engagement
5. Not letting staff know how decisions will be made	Before making key decisions affecting staff, whenever possible let staff know how the decision will be made— either by: • No input—for those decisions under crisis or where staff do not have the requisite skills or care about the decision; • Input, but leader still decides—for those decisions requiring feedback from others; • Consensus—for those decisions requiring a group mind-set; or • Others decide, with or without the leader involvement—for those decisions others need to learn by experience or the leader has no valuable input to add.

CHAPTER

MISALIGNED MOMENTUM
Rebound with
Rapid Redirecting

WHAT THE MISTAKE LOOKS LIKE

Sarah H. is an entrepreneur who started an information technology (IT) consulting business three years ago. Each year the company acquired more clients, leading to a booming business. Sarah H. had hired over thirty highly competent IT staff who were creative, risk taking, and full of energy. When a potential new client proposed an interesting project idea, several staff were eager to try something new. The client wanted Sarah's company to develop a product—a time card that would be scanned via fax and automatically posted to an organization's accounting system. It required using handprint recognition technology, which is presently not highly developed. Sarah assigned several

41

of her best people to the project, which took many more hours than she anticipated. The project team made slow progress because, in retrospect, this was not their true area of expertise. Eventually the project failed, and Sarah was not able to bill the client for any of the time the staff spent on product development.

Sarah realized she made a huge mistake. She took on a project that was not a good fit for her company's mission and core competencies. They were a service company, not a product development firm. By leading in the wrong direction, away from the organization's main business, she had created a major setback. A substantial amount of money was lost, and the morale of staff who participated on the project plummeted. In addition, other projects suffered because she drained them of the best staff resources. Sarah made a major strategic error.

THE CAUSES OF MISALIGNED MOMENTUM

Sarah became enamored with a project that interested her and her project team. When the client presented a challenging problem, she rushed to meet their needs and at the same time meet her own needs for demanding and interesting work. Sarah neglected to think back to the company's strategic plan priorities to determine if the project was in alignment.

If her team were passionate, in spite of the company priorities, Sarah could have sought approval for a direction shift. Because she didn't do this, time and resources were wasted on an effort that was not fruitful.

The mistake of *misaligned momentum—failure to align goals with strategic initiatives*—is likely to be made by leaders who are, by nature, independent and strong-willed. They're off on their own agenda rather than that of the organization. While this may work well in some contexts, this mistake can provoke serious trouble when leaders forget they are working within an organization and must conform to the expected strategy. Author Douglas K. Smith (1999), in his book *Make Success Measurable!*, found that organizations are not organized if people in them pursue divergent, conflicting, and unrelated goals. To innovate, organizations tolerate some degree of deviation from stated goals, but too much entrepreneurial spirit leads to disaster when the leaders act as if they are free to do whatever tickles their fancy. The exception, of course, is the leader of an established "think tank" or research and development unit whose charge is to explore innovative ideas. But, even then, the leader must consider the mission and vision of the organization and work within those boundaries. When a leader, like Sarah, moves in a misaligned direction, she most often is viewed as lacking a team orientation, critical to success in today's organizations.

Misaligned momentum also occurs when the whole organization loses site of its core business. Tom Salonek, CEO and president of go-e-biz.com, related his experiences in an interview with us: "We tried to make a product, and we're a services company. We invested between 650 and 800 hours. It did not work."

Misaligned momentum was also the primary mistake Boris Miksic made. As CEO and owner of Cortec Corporation, as well as the recipient of the 2000 Ernst & Young Entrepreneur of the Year Award, Boris is not afraid of risks—weighing them out cautiously and opportunistically. His critical mistake occurred in the selling of his business. In Boris's own words, "I was thinking spontaneously, didn't listen to other key stakeholders, and pushed the limits without a vision. I didn't even know how to create a vision for myself or my organization. I operated without it and sold my business without adequate understanding of a vision. Selling my business was the wrong thing to do." Essentially, Boris didn't align the immediate goal of selling with the long-term vision of the organization. Not only did he not align his goal to the long-term vision; he didn't have this vision. We'll tell you later in this chapter how this tremendously talented and visionary leader recovered from this mistake.

In recent years many organizations have run amok by diversifying way beyond their core mission or strengths; the most pronounced examples of this come through mergers and acquisitions. There is strong, documented evidence about how many of these fail. In some large-scale studies, reported by such prestigious organizations as the London Business School and the Academy of Management Executive, anywhere between 50 percent and 75 percent of mergers and acquisitions fail to reach financial and strategic targets. There are many reasons for this, including a failure to successfully integrate the culture of the merged organizations into a meaningful "whole." However, before even considering the integration of the cultural aspects of the merged organization, many managers have shown a tendency to diversify into fields far from the organization's core, often through these mergers and acquisitions. Our focus here is on the leadership aspect of mergers and acquisitions—executives pushing for something that goes beyond the organization's core business. Problems emerge when the new business turns out to be loaded with problems no one knows how to solve. Eastman Kodak, for example, thrived for decades in its camera and film businesses and then moved into pharmaceuticals and consumer health products with dismal results. Subaru, in the late 1980s, decided to expand into mainstream midsize family sedans, moving away from their economically priced four-wheel drive vehicles. Jeep and Ford had them for lunch, and after seven straight years of losses in the United States, Subaru reverted to its original niche (Labich and de Llosa 1994).

We hope you understand our message here. We are *not* against mergers and acquisitions. Simply put, our research has discovered that leaders fail when they make decisions that are not in consideration of the core business. Mergers and acquisitions are just one example. Our point is that any decision needs to be aligned with the organization's core strategy.

Understanding the causes of the alignment problem is a first step to recovery. In this situation, what creates the link between the mistake and the rebound is the lesson learned. We could not have summed up this learning perspective better than with the quote from one of our interviewed leaders, Sue Strother, executive vice president of sales and marketing at Adaytum: "Because we considered a product that didn't line up with the vision of our company, it defocused us. . . . Our lesson learned was to avoid deviating from your vision focus if at all possible."

For a relevant example of this misalignment problem, consider Kmart—once a giant and envied retailer. It wasn't very long ago that Kmart dwarfed even Sears as a megaretailer. Marketing analyses documented that Kmart inspired the same loyalty as Wal-Mart. So what went wrong? Well, as you may surmise since we're in the misalignment chapter, Kmart had problems with strategy formulation and achievement. Kmart leaders seemed prone to accept the latest of strategy fads for quick fixes to their problems. And the situation got worse. It wasn't just strategy identification but strategy maintenance that became the crux of Kmart's problems. They could not seem to stick with a focused strategy. During the period of the 1980s, they strove to diversify with such big-name acquisitions as Borders Books and OfficeMax. After a few years, Kmart sold these acquisitions to accommodate the latest strategy of the day—to become more of a heavy discounter. And with the turn of the century, the strategy turned once more. Kmart leaders decided to put up their dukes to Wal-Mart and engage in price wars. They couldn't win against giant Wal-Mart. And the rest, as they say, is history.

Kmart filed for chapter 11 bankruptcy. Leaders here couldn't identify and align the company's resources around a vision. From the 1980s through the early 2000s, they were on a disaster course because of this misalignment.

We have taught our own clients some lessons about strategy that help provide additional explanations for what happened at Kmart. Once a leader decides on a particular direction and all resources are focused on it, it's really difficult to alter the course. It's tantamount to turning a shipping freighter around in fifty-foot waves. We are not saying that this can't be done. In fact, sometimes leaders do have to do this. However, in Kmart's case, leaders simply can't keep doing this. There's a day of reckoning, and it hit Kmart in the early start of the twenty-first century.

Lest we be perceived as overly harsh on Kmart, it is quite surprising that only 20 percent of the 160 executives researched by Charles Farkas and Suzy Wetlaufer in their book *Maximum Leadership: The World's CEOs Share Their Five Strategies for Success* (1996) thought of themselves as the organization's top strategist. While we think that leaders should be strategic, very few really are. And this may have been the case for Kmart—and many other organizations according to the data from Farkas and Wetlaufer. Executives often consider themselves their organization's head visionary guru. Some are. These authors' data give us a different view. Our research not only corroborates this, but also tells what leaders can do immediately to correct misaligned momentum.

REBOUND WITH RAPID REDIRECTING

We asked some of our interviewees to review the scenario describing Sarah's predicament. *Quickly* cutting her losses, they said, is the key to Sarah's recovery. Sue Strother described a similar debacle she faced and said, "I cut my losses early. You've got to not be afraid . . . even though you have spent a lot of money." It is crucial to pay attention to subtle signs that other leaders in the organization do not support your effort, then move quickly to assess and refocus. Since organizational resources are at stake when this problem lingers, salvation is achieved by a strategy that entails the courage to halt activity on the misaligned endeavor—even if those involved, other than the leader, are committed.

When encountering this type of problem, sidestep disaster by changing direction and putting your department's ship on course with the organization's vision.

1. Recognize and admit that you're heading in the wrong direction.

One of the most difficult aspects of rebounding from misaligned momentum is to admit you're going down the wrong path and drop what you are working on to change focus. This typically requires abandoning pet projects about which a leader and/or her team members may feel passionate, in order to spend time on the organization's priorities. One of the leadership coaches we interviewed told us that clients he has worked with fail to rebound when they think "that somehow the leader has to stand firm when the rest of the team is off course."

John Dasburg is the former CEO of Burger King and is now chairman, CEO, and co-owner of ASTAR Air Cargo. When reviewing the scenario about Sarah at the beginning of this chapter, he said, "Sarah should explain her misaligned momentum as an 'error in strategy' and that she should get everyone enrolled in a solution so it won't happen in the future—this is consensus management. Specifically, there should be a request for suggestions from her direct reports on how they can organize their decision making in the future to prevent or reduce the possibility of repeating a strategic-level error." Hazel O'Leary, President Clinton's former secretary of energy, concurred with what we heard from John Dasburg: "Own the mistake by telling others, in all honesty, you made the mistake."

In order to get yourself and others involved in assessing what went wrong, carefully review your organization's strategic priorities and plans. Kick yourself out of denial and be ruthless in analyzing the real benefit of your current work for the company's future. Perhaps there's a portion of a project that you can salvage due to its strategic alignment, but avoid hanging on just because of the effort you and your staff have extended. You have to let go. This is precisely what our previously discussed leader, CEO Boris Miksic, did. According to Boris, "I immediately assessed what was wrong with selling my business prematurely. I did this by benchmarking other leaders who were successful." I determined that I would buy back the business and promised myself I would always consider big-picture perspectives when running this new business." Successful at this buyback, Boris never lost sight of the need for alignment of goals with the organization's vision. He has had remarkable success in taking his business from a $2 million organization during his buyback in the mid-1980s to a $27 million corrosives-control industry today. So successful and visionary is Boris today, that he is being sought after to be in the parliament of his native Croatia, and is a viable contender for the presidency of Croatia.

As you adjust your focus, limit the number of initiatives you consider. Effectively focus on a few clear and specific activities, rather than scattering your energy broadly. Jack Welch of General Electric, for example, introduced only five major initiatives in eighteen years as CEO (Charan and Colvin 1999).

In *The Change Monsters* (2001), author Jeanie Daniel Duck describes how one of her clients rebounded from misaligned momentum. Joseph (pseudonym) was a newly appointed executive vice president of sales and marketing for an international firm. Ignoring a newly developed strategic plan that focused on team development across divisions, he downplayed the importance of his subunits working together within his division, reasoning that they were all separate units and rarely teamed up on projects. In fact, two of the business units were using different business models from the one agreed upon by the executive group. By allowing this to go on, Joseph's public lack of alignment was perceived as undermining the team effort and his personal credibility. After receiving feedback from Duck, who was serving as a consultant in the organization, Joseph decided to put a rebound strategy into effect. He called a meeting of his direct reports for the upcoming Saturday and asked Duck to facilitate. That day he arrived wrapped in a flag, announcing he hoped his attire would prevent him from being lynched or burned, given what he was about to say! Then he reviewed the company's vision, mission, and strategy and gave very specific examples of how each manager in the room, including himself, was engaged in misaligned activity and how they were undermining the company's change effort. When he finished, the group was stunned from the direct feedback, but acknowledged a need to realign. They spent the rest of the session outlining values and behaviors, then activities they would commit to in order to get back on track.

2. Present the facts to those above you as to what is not working and why.

What will be critical here is to rebuild your credibility by articulating a clear analysis proactively. Identify what went wrong before others have to bring it to your attention. Bringing together the whole management team to make your presentation assures everyone hears the same message. In making your rebound presentation, include these components:

a. An overview of your understanding of the company's strategic plan, including vision, mission, and priorities.

b. An overview of the work in which you and your staff have been engaged.

c. An analysis of the gap between "a" and "b" with acknowledgment of any salvageable projects.

d. Your plan to scratch misaligned work and discussion of what you will focus on instead.

e. A request for buy-in and an OK to move rapidly ahead in the newly stated direction.

Former Clinton administration secretary of energy Hazel O'Leary advised us that you get this buy-in by "asking for their help and relating that you need their ideas in how to recover." Think about it. The last time you made a major blunder at work, there is a high probability that you attempted to shift course on your own. This is not always prudent.

While discussing the scenario of go-e-biz.com described above, Tom Salonek explained, "We cut bait on the project and refocused on what we were—a service business, not a product business. While we were hoping there was light at the end of the tunnel, we kept thinking it would work out. We realized that not only were we spending time on something that wasn't working, but we were distracted from our core business—IT consulting services." Bingo! Pay close attention to the "we" word here.

3. Protect your staff from penalties.

When the plug is pulled on a misaligned initiative, the leader must do everything possible to ensure the staff involved are not punished for their efforts. Described as "cannibal organizations" in the book *Why Teams Don't Work* by H. Robbins and M. Finley (1995), leaders who sacrifice their staff by allowing them to take all the blame and subsequent consequences cannot expect to have an effective rebound process.

The former CEO of Burger King and now chairman, CEO, and co-owner of ASTAR Air Cargo, John Dasburg, also stressed that, "Sarah should make sure that no one below her is financially penalized if this can be avoided. It's very important in her position as a founder, which is a position of higher authority than an executive, that she goes out of her way to make sure that the people on the project don't get a smaller bonus than people who weren't put on the project. While not a full bonus, she has to come up with a compromise solution so that they are not penalized for her poor strategic leadership. She needs to mitigate the financial penalty to the people who were involved."

In addition to making sure no one is penalized for the mistake, Hazel O'Leary suggests a great self-effacing strategy. According to her, "You invest your energy in recovery, but take none of the credit for its success." We believe this is a crucial enhancement to this recovery strategy. It is important for others to see that the leader is giving credit where credit is due—to the team who has helped realize the recovery strategy.

Box 2.1 presents a summary of the rebound strategy for misaligned momentum.

BOX 2.1.

Summary of the Rebound Strategy for Misaligned Momentum: Rebound with Rapid Redirecting

1. Recognize and admit you're heading in the wrong direction.
2. Present the facts to those above you as to what is not working and why.
3. Protect your staff from penalties.

PROACTIVE HINDSIGHT

To reduce the probability of misaligned momentum from occurring, make sure you take the time to be visible and available to your staff, communicating informally as well as through more formal channels. This will help you discern staff needs and interests. Then don't exclusively delegate the work you regard as boring or mundane. Rather be open to assigning interesting and varied tasks that stimulate the development of talent. Also, include staff in decisions that affect them. Use the shared leadership continuum discussed in chapter 1.

CHAPTER

POLITICAL MISREAD
Rebound with
Rapid Repositioning

WHAT THE MISTAKE LOOKS LIKE

Jon C. is a new, young hospital CEO who has advanced quickly and has a strong vision for the future of the medical center he leads. Having developed an ambitious strategic plan with some input from the board and staff, he is moving forward confidently. His staff is very enthusiastic about the passion Jon conveys and they are fully aligned behind him. Jon has successfully built a strong internal team.

Within the past year, Jon has expended a great deal of financial resources on new equipment the staff has requested and on a remodel of the ER. While reviewing his budget a year ago, he recognized he was off course, but was confident things would get back on track, given his projection of increased patient utilization of the oncology and radiology services. Recently, Jon received his financial report, which clearly showed he was in deep financial difficulty. The patient revenues had, in fact, declined, and Jon was in trouble.

Jon went to the board to explain the now dismal financial picture. Some board members were infuriated. They fired questions at him: "Why didn't you inform us earlier?" "Why did you go beyond the budget projections when you were directed to stay within boundaries?" "On what data did you base your patient projections?" Jon's answers were less than adequate, and the board chair, a physician, took him to task, demanding he turn things around within six months or his days were numbered. A couple of the board members seemed more understanding and wanted to give Jon more time to work out the difficulties. Later, Jon would discover the board was divided in their support for him, creating two factions that often fought over major decisions. This was a group dynamic Jon had not been attuned to.

Jon realized he had made a big political blunder. He had not established strong relationships with members of the board. Since Jon was not a physician and the board chair was an M.D., Jon's credibility was usually in question, whether it was fair or not. Jon had not supplied the board with enough information in a timely manner, and now the financial problem had turned into a crisis. Jon realized he had been naive about organizational politics by not creating a strong upward link to the base of power and influence.

THE CAUSES OF POLITICAL MISREAD

Leaders who make the mistake of the *political misread—failure to accurately assess political dynamics—*typically do so for one of these three reasons: First, they may lack savvy, in that they have not developed the ability to assess the power and influence dynamics within their organizations. By staying too focused in their own work units, they have not climbed onto the balcony to view the entire stage and the important aspects of the organization culture, which indicate how things really get done. This was the cause of Jon C.'s mistake in not building effective board relationships or keeping them informed. As a new leader, Jon appeared unaware of the importance of political analysis. Second, some leaders know how to assess the dynamics, but they make mistakes by misanalysis, which may result in aligning with a coalition unable to support their initiatives or, worse yet, one intent on sabotaging the effort. Third, some leaders have accurately assessed their organization's politics, but choose to ignore them. Those who believe they can lead independently and do not build coalitions to support their leadership most often make this mistake. By bucking the system before establishing the extreme credibility needed to be independent, leaders who go down this path find themselves alone with no support. In our own consulting practices, some of the leaders we have coached have told us that they "refuse to play corporate politics." They see politics as a dirty word and herein lies the problem—their frame of reference. We are not saying that all political maneuverings in an organization are always good. Rather, a lack of political savvy to read a situation, misanalysis, and/or ignoring organizational politics are quick roads to disaster. What leaders do need to do is understand how devastating political misreads can be and, when engulfed in a political misread, how to weave their way out of it.

Listen to what one of our interviewed leaders told us about his own lack of political savvy. Scott Vrchota was a former partner of a biogenetic implant firm—responsible for the sales and marketing of these products. In our interview, he noted that the one mistake he had made that derailed his career was ignoring the power that politics could play in his success. "Being too vocal and honest with my two partners and the parent corporation about how the business should be managed blindsided me," Scott noted. Essentially, he ignored organizational politics. Most astute leaders know that being more politically tuned in to the situation may prevent disaster. And this is precisely what Scott said, "If I had more open communication at an early stage of issue development, as opposed to later, we could have been more successful here. I also needed to be more attuned to the fact that when I was asked for my feedback, at times they really didn't want an honest, direct response." Unfortunately, Scott's insights came too late and he did not recover; he bailed out without a graceful exit. What impressed us about Scott was the fact that he understood the power of politics, learned from this, and used this learning in his next leadership assignment—where he is highly successful at managing Health & Care Products/Services for Park Nicollet Health Services in Minneapolis. We have discovered that many of our other successful leaders whom we interviewed were self-effacing in the way Scott Vrchota was—understanding their mistake and doing something about it. Leadership development guru Warren Bennis (1989) has found that truly successful leaders know when and how to expose their vulnerabilities. This is something that Max DePree, former CEO of Herman Miller, Inc., has noted when people have asked about his gifts as a leader—vulnerability is key.

With some, the political misread can be the Sword of Damocles hanging over a leader's head. Consider Steven J. Heyer, the current president and COO of Coca-Cola, Co. In a very recent article that appeared in the *Wall Street Journal* (Terhune, McKay, and Lublin 2004), some are doubting his ability to be the next CEO of Coke because of his inability to read the political culture at Coke. Coke announced that it would conduct its first-ever external search for a new CEO. Why? Listen to this about Steve J. Heyer: "While few doubt the former entertainment and advertising executive's intelligence, an abrasive and aggressive management style has some directors questioning whether he fits their vision of a world-class leader who can't only lead the company to new heights but also embody the warm, benevolent image of its iconic soft-drink brand" (A4).

In our study, we also found a strong domino effect springing from a lack of political savvy. Left unattended, other areas within the leader's domain may begin to fall apart more readily. As one of our interviewed executive coaches, David Bachrach, expressed to us, "When a key cornerstone element fails, like the ethics of the organization, the entire superstructure of the organization falls down." That's why we encourage leaders to never, ever compromise their ethics and, if others within the organization do so, to act swiftly and do the right thing to right the wrong.

Box 3.1 provides a summary of the primary causes for the political misread.

THE REBOUND STRATEGY: RAPID REPOSITIONING

Now let's consider the recovery side of things. Much has been written about the significance of great leaders who align their political behaviors to the situation. Consider Daniel Goleman's groundbreaking work on emotional intelligence, which focuses on leaders'

BOX 3.1.

Summary of the Causes of Political Misread

1. Not attuned to the power of political relationship building
2. Inability to assess politics accurately
3. Ignoring politics

abilities to manage themselves and their relationships effectively. To Goleman, emotional intelligence is just as important as intellectual prowess. We agree with Goleman that political navigation is a dimension of emotional intelligence. In fact, his research dovetails with ours from the perspective that it's not necessarily intelligence that can significantly derail a leadership career. It's how effectively leaders relate to others, as well as understand themselves. The dilemma that we investigated is that leaders may not know what to do if they have committed a political misread as a result of not using their emotional intelligence. Exit stage left: stop political misreads. Enter stage right: reposition your frame of reference.

We use the term "reposition" to indicate that this is really an overhaul of your perceptions and actions. In this approach you'll see assessment, intermediate actions, and full-blown actions—all designed to be executed in a relatively brief period of time.

1. Analyze the political landscape.

In order to recover, a leader who has committed a political snafu will have to move at once to reposition political alignments with the big picture in mind. Conduct an analysis of the political misread to uncover how things really work and learn what elements of power and influence you've neglected. Hand-wringing and browbeating are wastes of time. So is blaming others. To assist you in this analysis, consider the questions delineated in box 3.2.

Here's how this analysis played out with one of the leaders we worked closely with in terms of a political misread that could have been a serious career derailer. Meet Ricki P. To protect this individual's identity, we have altered various components of this scenario; these alterations do not change the importance of the message we intend. Ricki came to one of us because she had kept at arm's length a critical group she needed to involve in a key decision. Ricki was the

---

BOX 3.2.

Critical Questions to Help Analyze
the Political Landscape

1. How does your organization measure success (e.g., by revenue, profit, attainment of measurable goals, service improvement)?
2. How much time is given for results to be obtained? Are short-term or long-term outcomes most valued?
3. What is the decision-making process (e.g., leader decides without any input, leader seeks input and then decides, leader seeks consensus, others decide)? What groups or individuals review options and how do they communicate?
4. How much risk is tolerated and what are the consequences for failed attempts? Are lessons learned incorporated into the failure mix or are hands slapped with a "don't-do-it-again" mentality?
5. What are the organization's core values (e.g., patients come first, employees are our most important asset, stockholders are number one) and which are realized, not only espoused?

---

program director of a department in a large university in New England. Like many professionals, an ad hoc team of professors wanted inclusion in a decision about the direction of a specific project Ricki managed. She ignored the team's views, but not intentionally. Ricki seemed to simply get caught in a whirlwind of activity that isolated the team from the crux of decision making. As Ricki told us, "I found I just got so focused here on the project that I didn't adequately consider whose toes I was stepping on or whose egos I was ignoring."

One of the interview questions that we asked of leaders related to how much control they had over the situation wherein they made the mistake. Our analysis revealed that leaders do have ultimate control over the politically misaligned momentum issue. Ricki did as well; she just refused to acknowledge its importance.

Ricki did discover that she needed the team's involvement and attempted to garner this by seeking their input on how to go forward once she had already made her decision. Wrong move. This didn't work because she ticked the team off so much that they didn't want to discuss this decision any longer. She was at her wit's end.

Ricki had contacted one of us to work with her on a quick recovery strategy. She told us that she believed the best strategy might be to drop back five and punt. What Ricki meant by this was to talk with the team regarding how she really wanted their input in moving forward with her decision. No! Instead, we recommended that she drop back and reassess. Let's follow this scenario through the various stages we outline below.

We suggested she start by analyzing the political scene through a series of structured questions noted in box 3.2. She had just alienated a team that she needed for a new project initiative. It isn't going to do any good to go in there and perform a "mea culpa" by now involving them in a project that they really don't care much about any longer. One of us helped Ricki survey the landscape of power and influence.

Initially, Ricki wanted to simply apologize to the group and move on by involving them in the next steps of the project. We suggested that she not do this. The reason? Political mismoves are failures over which leaders typically have extensive amounts of control. Follow them with an explanation, and it appears as an excuse. Why? Because the recipients of the leader's mistake do not see the mistake in political terms. Rather, they see it as everything but (e.g., the individual is incompetent, they have their own agenda, they're a lousy leader). The excuse tends to cloud the message and can even reverse the positive message intended. It would be much better for the leader to reposition herself—as we suggested Ricki do. Save the apologies for when they're really needed (see chapter 5 on the apology).

Now you're ready to get a quick organizational snapshot to reposition critical political alignments, using the wide-angle questions in box 3.2. It is important to remember that you would conduct this analysis for those "critical" situations where your career or organization's success might be at stake. Remember, that while these questions may be used proactively into the future, we have constructed them primarily as a means to assess the political climate ASAP—after your political blunder.

In serving as an executive coach to Ricki, one of us posed each of these questions to her. The two that really hit home for her were numbers 2 and 3. She discovered that long-term results were far more indelible than are short-term wins. While Ricki "sort of" knew this, she found our questioning powerful because it forced her to reevaluate and reposition her effort. She found it far better, based on this culture, to look to the future with a fresh view versus revisit the old project and try to resurrect it by involving others in follow-up actions.

In considering the other key question regarding decision making, Ricki discovered that while she thought that consensus was the operational mode needed, she found that another approach would work far more effectively. She said that because a quick decision was needed, she assumed that consensus would never work and that she just needed to proceed on her own. Well, right on the first count, but wrong on the second. While consensus would be unwieldy here, she could still involve others by seeking their input and then using this input toward a more collaborative decision. In our work with clients, we have discovered that successful leaders understand how to build coalitions—and do so seeking consensus whenever possible. Notice we say "whenever possible." While at times leaders should make decisions without consensus (e.g., during times of immediate crisis, when others really don't care about the issue or result), consensus is usually the preferred political route. Why? With the advent of so many teams being built across levels and disciplines in organizations today, there are intricate political landmines within team sandboxes. These need to be brought into everyone's field of vision, wrestled with, tampered with, and ultimately, decided upon.

However, in Ricki's scenario, consensus was not the best mode because of the expediency needed. She failed to take this into consideration and made the error of seeing decision making as absolute—either you use consensus or go it alone. She failed to consider an in-between position of seeking input. Our approach of forgetting what has happened in the past and moving forward was "like being doused with cold water on a hot summer day—it awakened my senses," as Ricki noted.

Finally, review your answers to profile your organization's culture—the way in which things really work in your organization. We find that leaders who are brought in from outside their current organization tend to make the gravest mistakes when they neglect this analysis and continue to operate in ways that worked for them in their previous context. Remember that each organization has a unique culture characterized by many unwritten rules, which must be learned by observation and guidance from credible mentors.

If you use this analysis to dull the razor's edge of your political blunder, you'll find that you'll have a greater probability of resurrecting your good name in the organization and more importantly, your future working relationships there. If not, you may find yourself on a treadmill where you'll find it difficult to move beyond the error—at least in the eyes of others.

2. Profile key individuals.

To continue your rebound strategy, take a close look at the organizational chart and grasp the lay of the land. Carefully note the names of key organizational leaders, especially those who control resources you need to succeed. In this era of information management, keep in mind that a resource is not only money—knowledge is also a basis for political power. We do not see power as a dirty word. Rather, it can be the basis for good decision making and help leaders understand bureaucracies and how problem solving gets done. Box 3.3 lists another series of robust questions designed to profile individuals with whom you must have key relationships with after your political gaffe.

You may discover that specific departments or types of professionals tend to rule the roost. In many of the health care organizations with which we work, for example, physicians wield a great deal of influence and any leader attempting to bring about change must, therefore, be strategically aligned with them. Typically, they are influenced most by an analytical, data-based argument that is founded on a highly credible source. Gaining their respect most often requires consistent presentation of accurate information in a logical manner.

Beware. David Krackhardt and Jeffrey Hanson caution in their 1993 *Harvard Business Review* article "Informal Networks: The Company Behind the Chart," that leaders who claim to understand informal networks are often wrong. While able to diagram accurately the social links of the handful of people closest to them, the assumptions some leaders have about people outside their immediate range of contact tends to be off the mark. They suggest increasing the accuracy of your analysis by looking at three types of relationship

BOX 3.3.

Core Questions to Profile Key Political Gurus in Your Organization

1. Which areas of the organization hold resources critical for my own area to succeed?

2. Which individuals have the power to potentially hold or release those resources to me?

3. Which method of influence is most successful in my organization? Observe influential staff members and ask:

   a. What approach do they appear to use most frequently? Do they present well-researched data in a logical, orderly manner? Or do they use vivid stories and examples that play to the listener's heartstrings?

   b. How have they gained credibility? What types of accomplishments have led to their success?

   c. What do they do to match their behavior to the organization's culture?

   d. What coalitions seem to exist and do people become part of them?

networks: those on whom others depend for advice to solve problems, those whom others trust enough to share sensitive information, and those who talk frequently about work-related subjects. Now, think about yourself. Whom do you talk with frequently? Go to for advice? Trust? Look for gaps between your current network and a more influential one.

Let's continue with our scenario previously explored by demonstrating how Ricki used these questions to position her recovery.

Question 2 ("Which individuals have the power to potentially hold or release those resources to me?") of this second phase was one that "hit me between the eyes," Ricki quipped. This question helped her determine that there were two individuals she had observed who were "champions" of the team she needed to influence. Before this analysis, Ricki viewed the main stage as the entire group; after, she saw the need to influence these two key coalition members. Hold on to this reflection for just a moment longer as we proceed to the third step; we'll come back and use this concept of the champion in just a bit.

3. Build your alliance.

Build an alliance with one or more persons who will support your rebound effort. Try to find those who still have confidence in your abilities and also are influential in the organization. Seek their advice on how to proceed. Partner with them whenever possible to "learn the ropes" of the political landscape. This is precisely what Gregg Steinhafel, president of Target Stores related to us in response to the opening scenario in this chapter: "Jon should partner more with the board over the next six months." The partnership concept was corroborated in another interview we had with Leonard Schaeffer, who is the chairman and CEO of WellPoint. He is one of the top twenty-five managers in the world according to *BusinessWeek* (January 8, 2001), and WellPoint has been on Fortune's list of the most admired companies in America for five years running. In addition, WellPoint was named by *Forbes* magazine to their 2004 Platinum 400 Honor Roll of the twenty-five best-managed companies in America and has been on the list since its inception in 1999. It was also named one of the top four companies for executive women by the National Association for the Female Executives for the fifth consecutive year. Most recently, WellPoint's outstanding performance by Leonard Schaeffer as CEO was demonstrated by its ranking as the number three best performer in the *Business Week* Fifty, in which the top-performing 50 of 500 companies were listed ("The *Business Week* Fifty," *Business Week*, 105). In our interview with Leonard, he saw the primary short-term strategy in the opening scenario of this chapter as one in which the leader needed to establish a presence with his board by reaching out to them—making his problem theirs by seeking their advice.

And how about Ricki? How did she engage in this alliance-building process? We suggested to her that she seek out the champions we helped her discover in step 2 and seek their advice on how to proceed. Rather than going it alone, Ricki learned about newfound support she thought had long gone by the wayside. And surprisingly, Ricki discovered what we had been trying to help her understand— don't try to go back on your decision; look to the future.

At this point, some of you may be thinking that this does not appear all that "immediate." "It takes too much time," you might say. We have two responses to this. First, it is much more immediate than what some leaders typically do: overlook the importance of political dynamics and wallow in never-never land. Nonacknowledgment wastes precious time when actions are needed. Second, we suggest that leaders who make the political blunder act quickly, but not rashly. While the responses to this point take time, leaders who recover well here make this a top priority and proceed with a vengeance.

4. Rebuild relationships.

This is more long term. First, work steadfastly to build relationships with key people through individual conversations and offer them assistance in ways that will showcase your competence or that of your staff. This will require setting up formal and informal meetings with your "constituents" to discuss your activities and the activities they are involved in. Look for mutual interests and ways you can help them achieve their goals. This was one of the strategies suggested by President Clinton's former secretary of energy, Hazel O'Leary. At times being perceived by the media as perhaps "too bold and aggressive," she discovered the fine art of "common interests"— looking for content to pull the media away from her supposed overassertiveness. As you work each day, think about who would benefit from being informed about the things you are working on. Keep key people up to date and engaged in your projects. "Schmoozing," while distasteful to some, is an important dynamic for information gathering and relationship building. As you chat with others, use the encounters to gather information, staying up to date with hot organizational topics. Our experiences with the leaders we coach suggest those who stay removed from the informal communication often are left with their head in the sand, blindsided by developments that sometimes derail their own and others' careers. This is precisely the wisdom that Hazel O'Leary shared with us regarding the controversy of her first-class travel "paid" by the U.S. government. While Hazel noted the inaccuracy of this perception, she did nothing in either formal or informal communication to right the situation. As she noted, "I never tried to meet the distortions of truth, nor explain what I did. It still bothers my family and me beyond words." Her strategy was not to give the story "legs." This turned into a disastrous situation for Hazel, who eventually left office. She did not share with the media that she subsidized the first-class travel with her own funds because she was traveling with CEOs and other dignitaries.

Consider gathering together a group of your colleagues who are outside your immediate department to gain a clear perspective of their needs and wants. Put yourself as well as your staff in touch with others to build stronger alliances, improving communication and understanding.

And back to Ricki P. What one of us encouraged her to do was to take these champions she identified in phase 1 and begin building a relationship with them. Rather than going to the entire team right away, she first contacted these champions and helped them understand that she is firmly competent in a number of areas related to the project she flopped in. This was not only instrumental in building the champions' confidence in her, but also served as a catalyst for the champions sharing with other key stakeholders the competence Ricki possesses. Notice that Ricki has focused on her current competence. Just as important is for Ricki to look to the future.

5. Look to a future project.

Look for a juicy, challenging project to sink your teeth into, ideally one that has high visibility to show others you're on the fast track to success. Remember, your competence at the task was never in question; it was your competence at political maneuvering where the rubber met the road. So now that you are no longer on a political treadmill, you're well versed to take on that next big project. Go for it. Your newfound political savvy linked with your know-how is a winning combination.

Ricki P. did just this. With her newfound confidence, she tackled a project that helped her showcase her competencies that she let fall by the wayside previously.

6. Don't take the credit; give it away!

At this stage of the game it is so easy to rest on your laurels. Just remember you may need these alliances and relationships in the future. We have found that one of the best ways to keep relationships is to give away the credit. Trust us; you'll still receive the kudos for a project well done. It's just that now you'll have a cadre of people to rely on in the future when political maneuverings are needed. You'll have the context for setting this in motion with greater ease and success.

With your successful rebound accomplished, you're ready to tackle most new situations, and demonstrate political savvy by strong alignment of your behavior with the organization's culture. Don't make the same mistake twice or your chances of rebounding will be minimized. Regaining trust and credibility will require consistency and predictability, drawing on the informal network as a key communication tool. Box 3.4 provides a synopsis of this process of working your way through the political jungle.

PROACTIVE HINDSIGHT

One primary strategy is most effective in avoiding the political misread: Build a broad network of relationships, thereby creating a base of support and a wealth of resources to assist you in accomplishing

---

BOX 3.4.

Summary of the Rebound Strategy for Political Misread: Rebound with Rapid Repositioning

1. Analyze the political landscape.
2. Profile key individuals.
3. Build your alliance.
4. Rebuild relationships.
5. Look to a future project.
6. Don't take the credit; give it away!

your goals. We have found that successful leaders never underestimate the power of these relationships. With this network, many leaders have avoided the political misread, but you have to spot the road signs to really make this effective. What we mean by this is to look at the causes of the political misread—ask a special network of colleagues to provide feedback on how effectively you assess political dynamics. One of the best places to do this is at meetings. We have coached leaders to ask two or more trusted colleagues to give feedback on the leaders' political savvy. We even coach leaders with the causes of the political misread; these can also serve as prompts for the colleagues at the observed meetings.

In our role as consultants, we have also provided feedback to our client leaders as we observe them interacting with others. This is a viable strategy, particularly if the consultant has been retained to help build the team, engage in strategic planning, or develop leaders. In any of these contexts, there are ample opportunities for the leader to be observed.

Please remember that if proactive hindsight is going to be effective for the political misread, feedback is critical. And it needs to be honest, behaviorally specific, and direct.

CHAPTER

TOO MUCH, TOO SOON
Rebound with Rapid Reinventing

WHAT THE MISTAKE LOOKS LIKE

Ron A. has been a leader all of his life. From an early age, he's found himself in leadership roles in school activities and community events, and now, at age twenty-nine, he was asked to accept the principalship in a mid-sized suburban high school. Ron had been a coach and teacher for four years, and for one year, the high school assistant principal. He is well known in the community for his winning teams and as a top-notch tenth-grade history teacher. As assistant principal he skillfully handled an array of disciplinary problems and got the school climate back under control after many years of lax leadership. Always an excellent student, Ron completed his graduate degree at age twenty-five.

Things took a turn for the worst after Ron's first couple of months in the principalship role. The school district staff described Ron's leadership style as "bulldozer": abrasive, directive, autocratic, and, at times, insensitive to others. He has developed an arrogance that causes others to feel they are not valued and appreciated by him. Ron's lack of experience shows in his misunderstanding of district policies, school financing, and legal implications of decisions. The staff, many of whom are long-term employees, call him "the kid" and do not really respect his authority. The school board has shown concern with some of the curriculum changes Ron is championing, feeling they are too restrictive and conservative, lacking in creativity and innovation, which the community feels are important. Recently Ron violated a district policy in handling a teacher disciplinary situation, and the teacher is threatening a big lawsuit, which the district will most likely lose. Ron's job, and subsequent career, are now at risk.

THE CAUSES OF TOO MUCH, TOO SOON

Ron realizes he has made a critical mistake in accepting a position for which he wasn't ready. Enamored by the flattery of being asked at such a young age to assume the principal's role, he moved ahead too quickly and now is paying a huge price. He has made multiple errors of judgment and adopted a style that has alienated many of the staff who could have helped him through this initial learning period. Ron made a mistake that Richard Chant, principal of Wellington Search, says is often a career derailer for young, bright people. "Companies are willing to hire bright people. The assumption is that someone is a fast achiever because they are younger. I don't think someone will slow down on their own until they hit a wall." Shooting stars, like Ron, who fail early in their careers often do so because they do not have enough self-awareness to recognize they are in trouble until they run into something they can't do and fail. We call this critical error *too much, too soon—failure to identify personal readiness level for a given assignment.*

The U.S. Department of Labor shows a continuing escalation of employees aged twenty to thirty-four in management jobs. Even more surprising, Dun & Bradstreet reports that roughly 15 percent of managers in their twenties and thirties hold positions as CEO, president, and business owner. Many are thrust in the role with little preparation and receive minimal training once they are on the job (McDermott, *Training and Development*, October 2001). Because there is a greater need for middle-management talent than there was in the past, these new entrants to management have less professional grooming than their older colleagues.

Morgan McCall argues in *High Flyers* (1998) that leadership ability can be learned in an environment that supports the development of talent—becoming an organization's competitive advantage. However, he says, aspiring leaders often engage in the things that work against their growth. For example, they may receive ongoing kudos for their brilliant work. Unfortunately, their brilliance at the sophisticated competencies needed for their current jobs will not be a primary driver in their newfound management positions. As a result, it is easy for them to believe they are as good as everyone says and not take their weaknesses as seriously as they should. They may rely too much on their existing strengths and not develop the new skills they need to master a new position. We know this from our examination of inappropriate promotions. There is strong evidence that there is a tendency to promote based on current competence, not future needs. Just look around you at some of the newly appointed leaders in your organization. Our educated guess is that a number of them were really superb experts in their fields. After promotion, however, some are likely floundering because they don't have the prerequisite skills needed for their leadership position.

Before anyone jumps to conclusions here, we are certainly not saying that these previous scenarios only happen to younger folks. Our point is that it appears to occur with greater frequency among those new to the management field. This mistake is a red flag to leaders of any age.

Leaders must take responsibility for their own management development, even though the organization may focus little on adequate development planning. According to the research of McCall and Lombardo (1983), many individuals (both younger and older) who soar to the top and then fail demonstrate the following:

- A strong track record of bottom-line results
- Unusual intelligence
- Solid organizational loyalty and commitment
- Self-sacrifice in the generous amount of time they give the organization
- Charisma in both charm and ambition

Leaders face derailment when these demonstrated strengths transform to weaknesses. Their track record may be in a narrow area that blinds the fast-tracked leaders to the needs of the larger organization playing field. Consider Jeff Skilling, former CEO of Enron. His initial successes in leading Enron to highly profitable results certainly were a key variable that allowed his leadership style—that some have dubbed "arrogance"—to go on far too long. His approach was easy to "forgive" because of Enron's might in the profit arena. Staff members are highly unlikely to give meaningful feedback to leaders who "know it all" and are perceived as unwilling to accept criticism. We once saw a CEO become so upset with the feedback one of his staff gave him that he kicked the leg of the table several times, muttering a few profanities along the way. Trust us, this staff person never opened his mouth to criticize again!

Another drawback of leaders being quite brilliant is that it can cause them to quickly dismiss other people's ideas as not worthy of their attention. Organizational commitment can result in defining one's whole existence in light of work and demanding that others do the same. Charm can become manipulation. Excess ambition may lead to one doing whatever is necessary to succeed, even at the expense of people and the organization. Perfectionism, once perceived as the crux of overachievement, can be viewed as downright obsession with work—stifling creativity in self and others because everyone is afraid of taking any risks.

Leaders who make the too-much-too-soon mistake overestimate their own abilities. And, as with the discussion on emotional intelligence, we have found that it's usually their nontechnical skills that are overestimated. These kinds of leaders often take a quantum leap regarding their self-awareness and relationship skills from the perspective that either they have these under the belts or these "touchy-feely" skills are not especially important.

Now let's reconsider our original scenario with principal Ron. In the absence of self-awareness and organizationally endorsed leadership development, someone with talent, like Ron, can quickly get off track and risk failure. A strength that is no longer relevant to the new position can actually become a liability. A weakness that was not particularly problematic now becomes a bigger liability.

Lack of emotional maturity is also a reason young leaders promoted too quickly derail. They don't have adequate time to learn how to develop effective relationships, particularly with upper-level leaders. Many technical professionals who are promoted based on their technical skills alone may lack necessary interpersonal skills to work successfully with a complex network of organizational relationships at all levels. Research by Goldsmith (August 2003) suggests that the more we achieve, the more we want to be right, desiring our position to prevail. Therefore, listening behavior is decreased and attention to ideas not congruent with those of the leader causes relationships to crumble as people feel discounted.

THE REBOUND STRATEGY: RAPID REINVENTING

The focal point of this rebound strategy is sequential—from reducing visibility, to learning through an aggressive learning pattern, and finally to stepping up your visibility once again. We have discovered that a phased strategy to reassessing your skills works best here with the ultimate goal being a reinvention of your leadership self with a new approach. Our suggested initiation into this rebound strategy is to minimize key interactions, as we indicate below.

1. Quickly decrease your interactions and visibility with those who have been alienated by your approach.

Allow old wounds to begin to heal. Be visible enough to let people know you are meeting your obligations, but avoid any new endeavors or avoidable conflict that would shine the spotlight in your direction. Think of your style during this period as "understated." Cease and desist your failure-making behaviors while you complete the rest of this rapid rebound strategy. Unfortunately, we have found many leaders do just the opposite when they are found in the too-much-too-soon quagmire. Their impulses drive them into overkill as they engage in any or all of the following fruitless behaviors at this stage of the recovery cycle:

- Seeking excessive confirmation from nonalienated others to whom they tell (and retell) their story ad nauseum
- Hounding those whom the leader has alienated to provide rationalizations as to why they did what they did
- Changing their assumed alienation behaviors too quickly before they adequately understand what it is they did that drove others away

While the above strategies may indeed work at times, please remember that we are talking about a "critical mistake" that is a true career derailer. We're not addressing the everyday common variety of mistake here where a manager may have taken on a bit more than he or she can chew.

2. Seek advice from your own manager regarding position success.

Next, meet with your own manager to determine exactly how success in your position is defined. Make sure you understand the outcomes expected of you and how they will be measured. Indicate that you need assistance to succeed and request approval to ask others in the organization to serve as your mentor if your manager is not the most appropriate individual. While it may be difficult to admit you are floundering, it is necessary to put your ego aside for a moment and give your manager the opportunity to help you solve the crisis you have encountered by assuming a higher-level leadership role before you were adequately prepared. Do not blame your manager or the organization—even if blaming is justified. Remember, you are in a crisis mode and you want the quickest way out. Blaming is likely to put you on the endless road of what we term the "he said, she said" argument. While this may be important to do, it's not the right time. Sorting out the subtle nuances and details of the mistake is worthwhile, but not just yet.

3. Identify a mentor, along with 360-degree feedback at your side.

Find one or more experienced leaders who will serve as your mentors. Resist the urge to sign up for leadership development courses that will take way too much time to allow you to rapidly get back on a track to success. You need immediate individual counsel focused on your issues. Gregg Steinhafel, president of Target Stores, says regarding Ron: "He has to seek out key opinion leaders. You won't win others over without a select group who provide you with honest and direct feedback. He should identify a few internal advisors who would be willing to coach and mentor him. He is young, inexperienced, promoted too soon, and his style needs refinement. He has to find a way to gain the respect of the group. Ron has to depend on these people and use their instincts and guidance and defer to them a lot more than he has. He should have depended upon them more."

With your mentor(s) at your side, embark on the following rebound activities:

a. Get feedback from your own manager, your staff, and your peers, using a 360-degree assessment instrument. For those not familiar with 360-degree feedback, let us provide a brief look at this tool. In 360-degree feedback, leaders receive anonymous feedback from others who have significant experiences in working with them. Through a questionnaire (either online or on paper), respondents provide feedback to the leader based upon this individual's style, behavior, and effectiveness. Let us present a strong word of caution here. We recommend that 360-degree feedback in this context be used for development purposes, *not* performance evaluation. What we mean by this is that the results from the feedback should not be integrated into the individual's overall performance appraisal process or compensation structure. Remember, the individual who has made this critical mistake is initiating this to develop a bona fide action plan. It should be used in the most positive frame possible—not to appraise performance for compensation or personnel purposes.

b. Review the 360-degree feedback results. Look carefully at the results to pinpoint where you went wrong and determine what you need to do differently to reemerge with a new set of behaviors. Be open to learning about the gap between your perceptions of yourself and what the feedback reveals.

In our experiences using this methodology, you'll see results that validate what you already know and learn some things that may surprise you. Take it all in without defensiveness. Interviewee Boris Miksic, CEO and owner of Cortec Corporation and recipient of the Ernst & Young 2000 Entrepreneur of the Year Award, gave us some insight on this process. He said, "Slow down and take time to really listen to what people have to say to you. You need to hear the truth, not only what you want to hear. Be analytical in finding the cause of the problem. By going slow at first, your recovery will be faster because you will have focused on the right issues." And then really pinpoint one or two things you can do differently. Think of yourself as rapidly ascending from an individual contributor mindset to that of a leader who has the broad view, creating an environment that promotes talent utilization.

c. Develop a plan of corrective action and implement it immediately. With your mentor's assistance, identify specific action steps you can take to respond to the top problem areas noted in your feedback. Divide the action steps into those that can be accomplished quickly and those that will need more time to implement.

Make a list of all those you have alienated and prioritize those you are going to concentrate your attention on by earmarking who would be easiest to influence *and* have the greatest impact on your success. Go to these individuals with your action plan, detailing the changes you will make to rebound from the situation at hand. Ask for their support and counsel. Request that they provide some positive public relations for you as you begin making changes and others comment on what they see. This will begin the process of re-establishing your influence and credibility by surrounding yourself with a network of resources.

4. Within thirty days, increase your visibility within your organization with your new approach.

Remember that others will not immediately trust the changes you display, so be extremely consistent to regain credibility.

Gregg Steinhafel, president of Target Stores, relayed his own experience in making a too-much-too-soon type of mistake early in his career:

> I can remember early on when I was younger and newer to the position and didn't understand the value of the existing team's experiences and wisdom. I was an independent thinker and through naïveté undervalued their opinions and didn't get buy-in to the bigger cause. This occurred in my late twenties. I was promoted into a large and complex buying position somewhat prematurely and alienated a lot of people on my team. I alienated them because I didn't understand the value of each team member's contributions and didn't seek their opinions as often as I should have. I was too directive. I placed too great an emphasis on my own decision-making ability versus how to involve the team that had talent, skills, and insights. I didn't have a

lot of experience and didn't understand what the correct balance was between people and tasks and how to work through people versus just accomplish the goal. In this case I remember flashpoints with individuals, and it was through these times when there were heated exchanges. I recognized how passionate a couple of individuals were about the decisions and the direction we were going. I thought it would blow over, but it didn't. Then, the light bulb went on and I recognized how big an issue this was. I realized I would have to modify my behavior and approach in the future if I wanted to be successful within a large organization. The recovery was this: I made an abrupt change in my style. I admitted I was off base. I became much more collaborative, team-oriented, and empowering. I made fewer decisions independently and involved my team in the planning and objectives upfront—where we could have spirited dialogue and debate before we decided the course of action. People weighed in with their opinions. Also, after we made decisions I spent more time explaining the rationale behind those decisions and why we came to the conclusions we did instead of assuming everyone had fully grasped the complexities of the issues and were all on board. Accomplishing any goal is easier when the team fully participates in the objectives and feels accountable for the outcome.

Recovery from the too-much-too-soon error means reassessing one's skills with the help of a competent mentor and a leadership assessment tool that will help you profile what competencies you must develop. Eliciting and nondefensively receiving the feedback requires courage and the wholehearted willingness to change. Finally, leaders who make this mistake must emerge from the process of self scrutiny with a new set of behaviors designed to replace the old behaviors that caused the problem. We call this process "reinventing." Box 4.1 presents a summary of the rebound strategy for too much, too soon.

BOX 4.1.

Summary of the Rebound Strategy for Too Much, Too Soon: Rebound with Rapid Reinventing

1. Decrease your interactions and visibility quickly with those who have been alienated by your approach.
2. Seek advice from your own manager regarding position success.
3. Identify a mentor, along with 360-degree feedback at your side.
   a. Get feedback from your own manager, your staff, and your peers, using a 360-degree assessment instrument.
   b. Review the 360-degree feedback results.
   c. Develop a plan of corrective action and implement it immediately.
4. Within thirty days, increase your visibility within your organization with your new approach.

PROACTIVE HINDSIGHT

To reduce the probability of making the too-much-too-soon error, request feedback from others on your leadership skills. Consider using a 360-degree feedback process as outlined in this chapter. Request that your manager and/or other leaders in your organization help you assess if and when you have acquired the needed capabilities to move forward in your career. Pursue an aggressive leadership development process if you discover you have significant work to do.

MISCUED
DECISION MAKING
Rebound with
Rapid Redesigning

WHAT THE MISTAKE LOOKS LIKE

Dan S. is a high-level manager in the Wisconsin Forest Department with a wonderful record of service. He is currently in a helicopter flying over 25,000 acres of burned or burning woodlands. Dan authorized a "controlled" burn of 300 acres of dry and dead trees and brush two weeks ago. The burn was delayed because of an unexpected appearance by the state's governor. Four days ago Dan gave the go-ahead for the burn but neglected to review his staff's new weather and ground cover moisture information. Conditions had changed enough to allow the controlled fire to jump its boundaries and engulf over a third of the for-

est. To make matters worse, the fire has destroyed a historic Girl Scouts camp. The fire is almost under control, but many people are asking lots of questions.

THE CAUSES OF MISCUED DECISION MAKING

Information is the lifeblood of any leader. Poor or missing information results in bad decisions. Leaders make errors in judgment when they do not study important information and make decisions on limited facts. This is often due to the speed with which they must work and lack of knowledge about the situation around which they are making a decision. It may also be due to lack of adequate channels from which to receive information.

In 1995 many people thought that the software giant Microsoft had missed the boat. While the Internet was gaining dramatically increased usage, Microsoft seemed to ignore the impact this new technology would have on future markets. Wedded to the Windows operating system, which was very profitable, many of its leaders, including Bill Gates, were convinced that the future was in proprietary software that resided on the hard drives of customers' desktop computers. Suddenly, Bill Gates recognized the threat the Internet posed and headed off disaster by making a decision and taking immediate action. Outlining the company's new Internet strategy to the press and securities analysts in a "Pearl Harbor Day" briefing on December 7, 1995, he alone led an instant focus away from proprietary products and toward the Internet. Any project or plan that stood in the way of this new direction was cancelled, and every existing and future product had to be designed and built with the Internet in mind (Stoltz 2004).

It's not just the lack of or misuse of information that is a problem in poor decision making. Our own research indicates that it's also about using the right process for effective decisions. We call these critical errors *miscued decision making—failure to effectively utilize information or the right process.*

One of our interviewees, Ken Fry, president of Business Development for On the Scene Productions, Inc. in Los Angeles, described a flawed decision-making process he had mistakenly utilized to hire a sales representative: "The interview process was not as in-depth as it should have been. It was more based on the feelings of the owners of the company versus what I knew about this person. We didn't ask enough questions to discover if this person was a good fit for our organization. We ended up firing her because she wasn't qualified to do the work." Sound decision making needs to be based on the right process.

Consider this alarming statistic. According to a study of 356 decisions made in medium to large organizations, half the decisions in organizations fail (Nutt 1999). And the reasons? Leaders who

- impose solutions on others;
- limit the search for alternatives;
- use power to implement their decisions.

Sydney Finkelstein (2003) has identified several habits of highly unsuccessful executives. He says that the revered profile of the decisive leader making multiple decisions quickly, taking minutes to size up a situation and act, is bunk. Rather, his research demonstrates, leaders who make decisions this way rarely have an opportunity to grasp the ramifications. Because they often feel they have all the answers, they have no way to learn anything new and they do not seek out a variety of viewpoints. For example, Finkelstein says, CEO Wolfgang Schmitt of Rubbermaid was fond of demonstrating his ability to sort out difficult issues in a flash. He rarely heard differing viewpoints and arrogantly made most important decisions independently.

Three of the most common decision-making blunders include: (1) failure-prone practices, particularly lack of participation by others, (2) premature commitments stemming from jumping on the first idea that comes along, and (3) time and money spent on the wrong things, most often costly evaluations of ideas by outside consultants (Nutt 1999). The author also delineates several traps in the process that cause leaders to make bad decisions:

- Ignoring potential barriers to implementing decision
- Allowing ambiguous directions
- Limiting the search for solutions
- Failing to evaluate the risk/benefits of each option
- Overlooking ethical concerns and not learning from the decision-making experience

In contrast to bad decisions caused by moving too fast with limited information and a poor process, flawed decision making can also be caused by a leader being much too cautious. Former president Jimmy Carter has been described as using this approach. Data-driven, analytical, and focused on all the things that could go wrong, he was viewed by many as ineffectual in policy areas. Coming to a decision only after reading numerous reports that argued from differing viewpoints, he often vacillated between positions and was, therefore, viewed as indecisive (Dotlich 2003).

How do leaders know if their decision-making approach is overly cautious? Dotlich provides these criteria:

- You require second and third opinions before making any decision.
- You obsess about what might go wrong and become stuck.

- You believe every decision can have serious consequences.
- You don't give staff approval because you fear a proposed project is flawed.

One of our own interviewed leaders, Dr. Leo Ruberto, director of the American School in Qatar, spoke about a firing decision he made in a previous position in which he delayed too long: "I had the board support to remove a key staff person who was underperforming, but one of my close colleagues wanted to give him another chance and more time, promising to work with the problem staff person to alleviate the performance issues. I was in personal conflict with him and didn't have the energy, so I mistakenly gave the other administrator the time to work on the problem. The problem person falsified information, making me look bad and nearly costing me my job."

Some leaders make decision-making errors because they are inattentive to aspects of their environment that might be in their best interests to focus on. Typically, they are unaware of some of the internal trappings of how work gets done in a given area and, therefore, are not recognizing important information. The unawareness is based on assumptions about what is and is not important to attend to. While leaders cannot be expected to be well versed in every aspect of the operation they run, they must know enough to know what they may not know. This requires fully utilizing the resources that are available within and outside the organization. Recognizing important information that must be factored into decision making is crucial to effective leadership.

Sometimes leaders operate with old information, which at one time might have been accurate, but now is obsolete. Or information that might not have been useful in the past has more relevancy in the future. It did not occur to Coca-Cola leaders, for example, that a handful of complaints from children in Belgium could represent a major threat to the perceived value of its product in Europe. Johnson & Johnson, Cabletron, Levi Strauss, Nissan, Schwinn, and a host of other companies received requests from their customers for different product designs, but they neglected to see this information as an early warning sign that their customers were about to bolt (Finkelstein 2003).

Not only is their neglect caused by inadequate attention, they assume that the information is apparently inconsequential—when it, indeed, is not. The leader determines that something is not worth their attention or jumps to conclusions. Either response can be detrimental to a leader's career if it becomes a pattern or if the leader makes the mistake once too often.

From our research on the critical mistakes leaders make, three dimensions of flawed decision making stand out:

- Information is ineffectively used; and/or
- The process of decision making is flawed; and/or
- Relevant information is overlooked.

THE REBOUND STRATEGY:
REBOUND WITH RAPID REDESIGNING

Statisticians say that two-thirds of all decisions are bad ones. Surprisingly, successful leaders make the same number of mistakes as unsuccessful leaders, but they act quickly to cut their losses. As soon as they recognize their decision was bad, they immediately make a course correction to reduce the undesirable consequences. Less successful leaders take longer to acknowledge decision-making mistakes; some refuse to do so at all. Findings from *The Traits of Champions* by Wood and Tracy (2000) corroborate what we have discovered along with many others—immediacy for course correction is critical. Similarly, in *Failing Forward* (2000), author John Maxwell states that the difference between average people and achieving people, in general, is their perception of, and response to, failure. Our phased approach to recovery here is based on helping hundreds of leaders recover from flawed decision making, as well as the results of our own research study.

1. Acknowledge the error and take full responsibility.

Begin the road to recovery by acknowledging the error to those involved and taking full responsibility. In Dan's situation described in the opening paragraph of this chapter, he should go immediately to his own manager and admit he did not utilize adequate information and consequently delayed a decision that should have been made more quickly. When employing this step, make sure you adjust your attitude about the ineffective decision you have made. Avoid thinking of yourself as a failure. A bad decision is inevitable given the demands of complex organizations with many variables to take into account. Covering up the mistake or minimizing it will most likely lead to reduced credibility and, possibly, job loss. Acknowledging your responsibility for the mistake and taking quick action to correct it may ultimately be viewed as a strength for which you are admired.

2. Assemble a SWAT team.

Your next step is to quickly assemble a SWAT team to help you deal with the situation your poor decision has created. Select members based on the technical expertise they have that can help you analyze what went wrong and develop an array of potential strategies to correct the problem at hand. In Dan's case, he should immediately gather a group to develop the strategies for making sure the burn is completely controlled and stopped, then to devise a plan to ensure this mistake never happens again. They need to immerse themselves in a marathon, night and day if necessary, of solution creation and immediate action planning. A SWAT team can include outside consultants or experts who may be able to speed up the problem-solving process, especially if they have more experience than the immediate staff involved. The success of the SWAT team is crucial to an effective rebound and may result in your gaining accolades for fast action in a difficult moment. However, if the SWAT team fails or makes the consequences of the bad decision even worse, your mistake may be fatal to your career. Select members carefully.

3. Analyze what went wrong.

Once the crisis is resolved, move at once to analyze why you didn't have or use the needed information to make a better decision. Ask yourself the following questions:

- Am I focused on too many initiatives, making it difficult to drive decisions due to sheer volume?
- Do I keep track of all critical assignments delegated, tracking progress and staying on top of my game?
- Do I have adequate information available when I need to make a critical decision?
- Do the staff members who hold information I need understand when and in what form it should be communicated to me?
- Am I tapped into the informal communication networks within my organization to stay on the pulse of what staff members know and care about?
- Do I evaluate the efficacy of decisions I make and adjust my approach accordingly?

Based on the answers to these six key questions, develop your personalized approach to decision making to prevent further undue problems.

Next, draw from the research on what an effective set of decision-making steps entail, using the following steps:

a. Identify the problem. Pose a question, setting the tone for a discovery process. For example,

- What can we do to ensure we hire the right people the first time?
- What can we do to eliminate the employee parking problem we are now facing?

b. Determine the cause or causes of the problem. Avoid the classic error of leaping to solutions before understanding why the problem is occurring. This is the time for brainstorming in order to get all the potential causes out on the table. If you don't identify the true causes at this stage, your solution will be flawed.

c. Generate solutions. Poor decision makers identify one solution, locking onto it too early in the process. We know from the research of decision-making experts that considering several competing options improves the quality of decision making.

d. Apply criteria to analyze the options. Typical criteria with which to weigh each option might include cost, time to implement, staff resources needed, quality, appearance, and reliability.

e. Select an option. Base your selection on which option fared best in your analysis, meeting the criteria you established for decision making.

f. Implement. Take concrete steps to carry out your actions. When working with your emergency SWAT team, consider two classic recovery strategies for poor decisions: First, you might cut your losses. For example, this would require moving quickly to fire or buy out a bad hire, sever a contract with a poorly performing vendor, or sell off a building that is a financial drain. Cutting your losses is a form of damage control that limits further bad results from a poor decision. Second, you might explore compensating for a bad decision. For example, if loss of money is at stake, finding ways to replenish funds through another initiative may reduce the problem created by your bad decision. When one of the leaders we interviewed, Supenn Harrison, CEO and owner of Sawatdee Thai Restaurants in Minnesota, opened new restaurants in suburban and outstate locations, her company suffered significant financial loss. She attempted to sell the businesses as a way of cutting her losses, but was not able to find buyers. So she rapidly moved to compensate for the bad decision by paying all her staff their normal wages and not paying herself and her husband until the financial picture began to improve. Then, she began a marketing/education campaign offering cooking classes, a newsletter, and advertising that Thai food is healthy and delicious. Bad decisions were overcome, and the restaurants quickly got back into the black.

Dorothy Dolphin, chair of the board of Dolphin Holdings (consisting of 21st Century Bank and Affiliates, Dolphin Fast Food Division, and Dolphin Temporary Help Services), recounted in her interview with us a time when her leadership team was too slow in getting the Management Information System (MIS) department running: "Once we realized we were lagging behind our competition in utilizing technology, we began to move rapidly. The board quickly allocated more resources, and we carefully monitored our personnel to make sure they were doing what was needed. The agency has since constructed an MIS department that is ready to meet future business needs."

g. Evaluate the effectiveness of the results obtained. This step will be crucial in helping you reduce the odds of making a poor decision again. A good decision-making process should include an attempt to see the problem and ultimate solution with different lenses. Get multiple views, then evaluate. One example of this not occurring is with former General Motors CEO Roger Smith. Roger Smith was purported to rid the firm of executives, or even board members, who didn't see eye to eye with him on critical issues. He did this by firing them or sending them to areas where they could not significantly influence the firm.

4. Make sure you know and can articulate what information is important to your decision making.

If you've neglected to detect important information, causing you to make a flawed decision, move at once to find a reliable informant— an individual who can help you in discerning what you failed to uncover and why. Make sure you ask detailed questions to get a clear understanding of the information required in your organization to make an informed decision, anticipating the explanations you will have to provide to your own leader and, in some cases, to the public. You must be able to articulate clearly about what you neglected to provide in order to let others know that you have learned from the mistake and educated yourself on the issue. In some cases, you may want to have an expert at your side to justify your negligence by indicating the complexity of the issue and the ease with which one could overlook and articulate information. Box 5.1 provides a sample list of questions you might consider asking this resource person.

BOX 5.1.

Sample Questions to Consider
Asking the Reliable Informant

1. Were there any written rules that I violated? Which ones?
2. Were there any unwritten rules that I violated? What were they? How should I have known these rules?
3. Are people reluctant to give me critical information? If so, why?
4. Do I pay attention to the wrong things? If so, what?
5. Do I ask enough questions? If not, what kind do I need to ask?
6. Do I build relationships with my team? If not, what prevents this from occurring?
7. Am I an information bottleneck? If yes, what do I do that causes people to perceive this situation, and hence, not flow information through me?

Before getting someone to agree to be your reliable informant, make sure they understand the role you are requesting them to fill. Give him or her the list before they agree to accept this confidential spot with you. Give them some time to reflect.

If you enlist them as your reliable informant, listen! And demonstrate your listening by writing some of the feedback down. They'll be impressed with your conscientiousness to really do something about the situation, and you'll get significantly more meaningful data.

Remember the Space Shuttle Challenger and Columbia explosions? NASA's tremendous hierarchy was a catalyst. When staff reported problems to supervisors, they, in turn, could choose what to do with this information. To make matters worse, supervisors did not have the permission to garner information from those who were not in their direct report command. Thus, tragedy struck.

Miscued decision making requires rapid action by analyzing what went wrong, apologizing for errors that impact others in the organization or constituent groups, then assembling a group of people to find the best immediate solution. If failure to uncover adequate information is the culprit, analyze your information-detection capability and revamp your information input process.

5. Apologize.

When the consequences of poor decisions negatively affect the staff you lead or the public you serve, an apology is in order. Not just *any* apology will do, however. Without sincerity and careful thought, an apology can do more harm than good. U.S. Senate Majority Leader Trent Lott, at a televised national event in December 2002, stated that the nation "wouldn't have had all these problems" if Senator Strom Thurmond had been elected president in 1948 when he ran on the segregationist Dixiecrat platform. During the following two weeks, Lott apologized several times, but his words had little impact. He said, "I take full responsibility for my remarks. . . . I only hope that people will find it in their hearts to forgive me for that grievous mistake." His apology, viewed as weak and lacking any attempt at rectification, was not accepted, and he announced his resignation as majority leader of the United States Senate for the 108th Congress. Other lackluster apologies that just didn't cut it include:

- Gary Hart, after his presidential bid collapsed in 1987 over a tryst with Donna Rice: " I am . . . deeply sorry. . . . I exercised bad judgment, but . . . not as bad as some others."
- President Richard Nixon in his 1974 resignation speech: "I regret deeply any injuries that may have been done. . . . I would say only

that if some of my judgments were wrong . . . they were made in what I believed . . . to be in the best interest of the nation."

- Roseanne Barr, after President George H. Bush criticized the way she sang the national anthem: "Well, I'm sorry I didn't sing so good, but I'd like to hear him sing it."

These apologies don't pass muster because the audience to whom they were directed just didn't believe that they were sincere. Too weak and lacking any statement of corrective action, the words fall short of winning back the confidence of those offended.

Our research suggests that the best leaders know how to apologize. And it's not the way we in Western society typically apologize. Here is the *wrong* way that is common to our society, summarized in box 5.2.

a. The *wrong* way to apologize

1) Offer a statement of regret.

Here the leader begins the sequence with the actual apology. It usually begins with the words "I'm sorry about . . ." or "I apologize for . . ." Consider the resignation of Cardinal Bernard Law of Boston, who resigned his position as the most powerful Catholic archbishop in America and asked forgiveness in the wake of the spreading sexual abuse scandal. He said, "To all those who have suffered from my

---

BOX 5.2.

The Wrong Way to Apologize

1. Offer a statement of regret.
2. Follow the statement of regret with the word "but."

shortcomings and mistakes, I both apologize and from them beg forgiveness." International expert on apologies, Aaron Lazare, chancellor of the University of Massachusetts Medical School, analyzed this apology by noting Cardinal Law did not fully acknowledge what he did. He should have admitted that the problem is embedded in the Church's culture and specified who the audience of offended people were. Additionally, he should have laid out a plan by which he would do specific things to rectify the situation (Allen 2002).

2) Follow the statement of regret with the word "but."

After the apology, the ineffective leader uses the word "but." Using the scenario above, we'll attach this additional word here: "I'm really sorry, but my hands were tied and I couldn't consult the rest of you before I made this decision."

Do you see what happened? Let's answer this by considering what communication experts have discovered about this typical kind of apology. First, by following the actual apology with the word "but," it does not appear sincere—almost akin to the fact that the leader really doesn't believe this. And second, what follows the word "but" becomes the excuse. In this case since it's the last thing the listener hears, there is a greater tendency to remember the excuse and forget the apology.

To be effective, an apology must include four essential parts, which add depth and commitment to change to the message delivered. Here is our four-phase apology model, summarized in box 5.3.

b. The correct way to apologize

1) Acknowledge the mistake made, framed in the past.

Clearly state the mistake made: "You all know what happened last week. I didn't have all the necessary information at hand when I decided to abort our contract with Evener Engineering. I know most of you thought it was the wrong decision, and I realize now you were right. The turmoil caused by severing the long-standing

> BOX 5.3.
>
> ## The Correct Way to Apologize for Your Action
>
> 1. Acknowledge the mistake made, framed in the past.
> 2. State how your action affected others.
> 3. Say you are sorry.
> 4. Indicate how you will rectify the situation.

relationship with Evener has caused us hundreds of hours of staff time in troubleshooting as well as financial strain."

Henry Paulson, Jr., chairman and CEO of the Goldman Sachs Group, provides a strong example of how to execute a successful apology. During a question-and-answer session at a Salomon Smith Barney conference, he said, "I don't want to sound heartless, but in almost every one of our businesses, there are 15 to 20 percent of the people who really add 80 percent of the value." His remarks angered employees who felt he was suggesting most of them were irrelevant to the company's success. Acting quickly, Paulson sent a voice mail message to all of Goldman's 20,000 employees apologizing for his "insensitive" and "glib" remarks. He knew he couldn't wait until the upcoming town hall employee meeting. He took full responsibility by acknowledging that what he said was offensive and "totally at odds with the way I really think about people here." He spoke sincerely and displayed humility, vowing to not make the mistake again (Gaines-Ross 2003).

2) State how your action affected others.

This is just as important as the acknowledgment because a question in many people's minds is whether you understand just how your action affected them. We recommend starting the empathy statement with "I." For example, "Everyone here has worked really hard to deal with the situation, and I know how frustrating it has been. Many of you have shared your concerns, and I've observed the extreme effort you've put forth and stress you've endured. I certainly understand if you are disappointed or even angry with me."

3) Say you are sorry.

Here, you simply add the tried-and-true mantra of either "I'm sorry" or "I apologize" to the previous statement. "I apologize to all of you for making the wrong call in not renewing the contract with Evener."

4) Indicate how you will rectify the situation.

This is often a missing step in poor apologies. In deciding what you can do to rectify the situation, consider that your solution must satisfy the offended party. It can't always be what's convenient for you: "I have started negotiations with Evener and will reinstate their contract within the next thirty days. I want to thank all of you for your feedback and attempt to work with the situation. We will be back on track shortly."

While we've placed the guidelines for making effective apologies in this chapter, this rebound strategy can be utilized with any of the mistakes we've identified if the impact constitutes harm to others.

Box 5.4 provides a summary of the recovery strategy for miscued decision making.

PROACTIVE HINDSIGHT

Miscued decision making can be avoided. One of the best strategies for doing this is to be certain you are using brainstorming methods involving others whenever possible. Avoid limiting alternatives too early in the decision-making process. Delay critiquing until options have been generated, then carefully analyze them, utilizing criteria for what constitutes a good outcome. Make sure your decisions are based on data from reliable sources.

BOX 5.4.

Summary of the Rebound Strategy for Miscued Decision Making: Rebound with Rapid Redesigning

1. Acknowledge the error and take full responsibility.
2. Assemble a SWAT team.
3. Analyze what went wrong.
   a. Identify the problem.
   b. Determine the cause(s) of the problem.
   c. Generate solutions.
   d. Apply criteria to analyze the options.
   e. Select an option.
   f. Implement.
   g. Evaluate the effectiveness of the results obtained.
4. Make sure you know what information is important to your decision making.
5. Apologize (the correct way).
   a. Acknowledge the mistake made, framed in the past.
   b. State how your actions affected others.
   c. Say you are sorry.
   d. Indicate how you will rectify the situation.

CHAPTER

6

STIFLED COMMUNICATION
Rebound with
Rapid Releasing

WHAT THE MISTAKE LOOKS LIKE

A number of people are very sick throughout the region in which Jane P. does business. It turns out that her company's frozen pizzas are what is making them ill. Jane's plant manager cites a clean bill of health from the latest federal food production inspection, so she blames her cheese supplier, and the problem seems to go away.

However, disgruntled employees leak information that shows the federal inspection report did list some minor problems that, if combined with continuous peak-capacity processing runs, could cause major contamination problems. The fact is, Jane has routinely ordered continuous over peak-capacity runs in order to increase profits. Her plant manager

comes to Jane and admits that this was the real problem that led to the
pizza contamination. He says he did not speak up before because he was
afraid of being fired.

While nothing has erupted at the moment and the previous prob-
lem with the pizza is under control, Jane realizes she has made a big
mistake in the way she has handled staff errors in the past.

THE CAUSES OF STIFLED COMMUNICATION

When leaders create a climate of fear, staff are often unwilling to reveal
their own shortcomings. We call this mistake *stifled communication—*
failure to create a work environment where staff openly communicate.
There are three causes of this situation:

- Punitive conditions
- Psychological distance
- Judgmental questioning

Punitive Conditions

The first cause is the situation where leaders are punitive in their
approach to managing others' errors and do not make it safe for staff
to be vulnerable. Punitive behaviors include giving harsh, critical
feedback that does not provide opportunities for correction; pulling
someone off a project without adequate direction on the leader's
part; giving an entirely poor performance review when only one
aspect of an individual's performance is at issue; and even firing the
offender for an innocent error. Staff who have experienced these
consequences or observed them being handed out to others soon
learn to be cautious in what they reveal to their leaders. They assume
protective behaviors, withholding information or covering up mistakes they have made for fear of undesirable consequences.

Creating an open communication climate is especially difficult for senior executives. Often they do not hear bad news because their staff is reluctant to be associated with a negative image of upper-level leadership. The phenomenon of withholding negative information as it passes up the organizational hierarchy has been termed the "mum effect." Honest feedback and accurate information become difficult to access; the leader can quickly become out of touch. In *Why Smart Executives Fail* (2003) author Sydney Finkelstein states that the problem of cover-ups is more common than most of us think. They occur most often in organizations where there is an illusion that theirs is a model, "dream" organization. This causes leaders to punish bearers of bad news who contradict this illusion; staff members become overly positive or at least "slant" the truth in the more positive direction. This "obscenely positive attitude that leads to cover-ups also causes the cover-ups themselves to be covered up" (177).

Staff mistakes sometimes occur because leaders make it difficult for them to ask for help. The staff are afraid of looking stupid. While crafting one of the mirrors for the Hubble Space Telescope in 1978, the team of top engineers at PerkinElmer made a 1.3-millimeter miscalculation. To make up for the error, they jammed three household washers onto a one-million-dollar lens. The world's leading optical scientists who were hired as consultants to prevent such mistakes never heard about the problem, so the world's most expensive mirror went into space before anyone realized it was flawed. What prevented the engineers from consulting the experts? They were afraid they would be considered incompetent if they depended on others for assistance. Apparently, impressing management becomes more important than getting needed assistance. These are fears—rational or not. What is critical is that leaders need to consider what they do to promote these fears. It is obviously far more productive for individuals to ask leaders for help rather than to fear retribution and subsequently not ask for assistance.

Creating a climate of trust and openness is no small task. Leaders must view mistakes made by their staff as learning experiences and adopt a style of debriefing and coaching, not punishing. Leaders must also adopt an open communication style by encouraging others to give them direct feedback on ideas and initiatives with which they don't agree. The New York Times Company, for example, has a cultural value statement which states, "Treat each other with honesty, respect and civility. Take risks and innovate, recognizing that failure occasionally occurs. Give and accept constructive feedback." Boeing has employed an "Ethics Hotline" to provide a way for staff to speak out and "Process Councils" to look at problems staff had—what worked and what didn't. General Electric has utilized a reverse mentoring program for junior managers to teach senior managers as a way of de-emphasizing the leadership hierarchy and opening communication. The Air Force uses a postmistake debrief process wherein the team at fault enters a room where no one else is allowed. The formal leader is just another member of the team and begins by acknowledging his or her part in the mistakes and asking others to provide feedback on leadership performance.

Psychological Distance

The second cause of the stifled communication mistake is one of psychological distance. This is the situation where staff tell you what you want to hear in order to avoid any close interactions with you. For example, consider the following questions in your quest to determine if you are a participant in the closed environment (box 6.1).

Judgmental Questioning

The third cause that stimulates the stifled communication mistake develops through the questions leaders ask. Questions can be open and

---

BOX 6.1.

Questions to Discern Psychological Distance Related to Stifled Communication Mistake

1. Do people appear to give you canned answers when they return your calls?
2. Do individuals avoid you?
3. How many people actively seek your input?

---

nonevaluative, or they may be closed and judgmental. Consider these hypothetical questions leaders may ask regarding poor client service:

- Why do you think the client reported a lack of responsiveness?
- Wouldn't you agree that there was a lack of responsiveness with this client?

In the first question, the leader is asking the question without any malicious intent. It is genuine information seeking. In the second question, it is a cross-examination that attempts to bring the other person to your side. It is deceptively persuasive because it is a statement disguised as a question.

THE REBOUND STRATEGY: REBOUND WITH RAPID RELEASING

1. Immediately assess your response style to staff mistakes.

Use table 6.1 as your guide to analyzing what elements of your approach are producing the defensive communication environment you have created. You may wish to engage the assistance of a leadership

TABLE 6.1.

The Leader's Style in Defensive vs. Open Communication Environments	
Defensive Communication:	**Open Communication:**
CLOSED NONVERBAL AFFECT	OPEN NONVERBAL AFFECT
Tight facial expressions	Relaxed facial expressions
Angry or tense voice tone	Conversational voice tone
EVALUATIVE WORD CHOICE	DESCRIPTIVE WORDS
You were stupid.	*I am concerned that our customer felt she received poor service.*
What were you thinking?	*What was your rationale for making this decision?*
You were insensitive to the client needs.	*The client reported that you interrupted her when she was trying to explain the situation. What's your perception?*
BLAMING AND SHAMING *This is all your fault.*	DISCUSSION OF THE CAUSE OF THE MISTAKE *Let's see if we can determine how this happened.*
THREATS OF CONSEQUENCES *If we lose this account, your career here will be seriously limited.*	JOINT PROBLEM SOLVING *Let's determine a strategy we can put into place to prevent us from losing the account.*
	DISCUSSION OF ACQUIRED LEARNING FROM THE MISTAKE *What did you learn from this mistake?*
	What will you do differently the next time this kind of situation occurs?

coach who can help you determine what you need to do differently and provide some practice activities. Remember that you must act quickly; this cannot be a long-term project. Work intensely on this step for several days, and then emerge ready to face your staff with the next recovery step.

2. Avoid blaming staff who did not fully communicate.

Once you recognize the style makeover you will need to pursue in order to rapidly recover from this mistake, hold your tongue and make sure you take full responsibility for the problem at hand. If your style had produced less defensive posturing on the part of your staff, you would now be more fully informed and the mistake would never have happened. In Jane P.'s case, she must be sure she does not slip into old behaviors that will derail the rest of her recovery strategy.

3. Prepare to defuse anger.

A closed environment has the strong tendency to ignite anger in others. In preparation for step 3 in this rapid rebound strategy, study and practice anger diffusion, following our guidelines. With our own organizational clients, we have shared a two-step process (box 6.2). Begin by empathizing and acknowledging feelings before trying to address the issues that caused the problem at hand. Make sure you don't overdo it here and appear condescending. Empathize with discretion and without being a parrot. For example, we have all heard the empathizing phrase, "I understand how you feel." It's overdone. Better to say something like, "If I were in your shoes, I'd feel the same way." Also, be sure to mirror the anger accurately. If a person is really upset, don't be trite by saying, "You sound concerned." No they don't; they sound really upset!

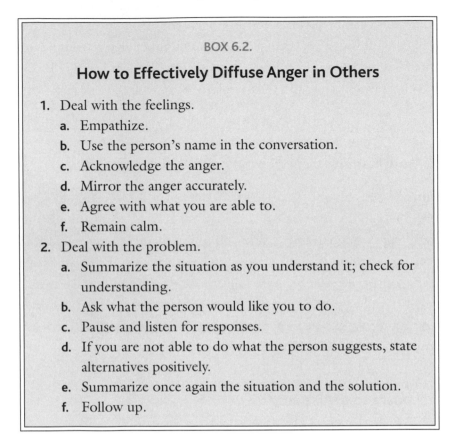

BOX 6.2.

How to Effectively Diffuse Anger in Others

1. Deal with the feelings.
   a. Empathize.
   b. Use the person's name in the conversation.
   c. Acknowledge the anger.
   d. Mirror the anger accurately.
   e. Agree with what you are able to.
   f. Remain calm.
2. Deal with the problem.
   a. Summarize the situation as you understand it; check for understanding.
   b. Ask what the person would like you to do.
   c. Pause and listen for responses.
   d. If you are not able to do what the person suggests, state alternatives positively.
   e. Summarize once again the situation and the solution.
   f. Follow up.

Agree with what you are able to: "If that's the way the situation seemed to you, I can see how you'd be upset right now," or, "That must have been a really tough way to start your day. I understand why this was so upsetting to you."

Now deal with the problem, following the steps we've delineated.

4. Meet with your staff to acknowledge the problem and present your plan for change.

You must plan carefully for this meeting in which you will admit the mistake you have made in adopting an ineffective communication approach. Consider the following agenda for this critical part of your rebound:

a. Thank the staff for being there.

b. Introduce your objective by stating you have thought carefully about your approach to communication with the group and have drawn some conclusions, which you would like to share.

c. Delineate and give examples of the communication approach you have used in the past, which you now know has been ineffective.

d. Check for understanding to see if you are on target. If not, listen and adjust.

e. State what you intend to do differently to keep the communication channels more open and to make staff more willing to give you information, including mistakes they have made or problems that are brewing in their areas of responsibility.

f. Indicate that you realize re-creating the communication climate will take time and say that you intend to check in with the group periodically to get their feedback on how things are progressing.

g. Ask for questions and comments. Utilize the process for diffusing anger presented in number 3 above, if needed. Thank the group for listening and restate your commitment to improving the communication. Ask for their support in solving the problem as a team.

5. Develop a process for dealing with information that includes more checks and balances and reward for those who reveal problem areas.

To complete your rapid rebound, you will need to review the current checks and balances within your department, determining what information you have asked staff to share, how frequently, and to whom. Assemble a group to assist you with this analysis. Invite select staff members and others from outside your area of responsibility who can give you an objective viewpoint. Working together, revise your checks and balances to ensure the communication process is not inhibiting information flow.

Now it's time to get creative. Think about how to reward your staff for revealing problems and mistakes. Minimally this should include giving verbal and written praise when mistakes are brought forward. To be even more overt, consider a cash reward or object of value, like the plant manager at the Wisconsin-based Quad Graphics who routinely gives teams who take risks and fail a case of champagne to reward their "failure" and celebrate the learning that stems from it. Rewarding the best mistake-recovery strategies of the individuals and teams you lead is crucial to putting the finishing touch on this rapid rebound strategy. The following statement may sound quite strange in this era of contingent rewards—you should be rewarding "failure" with the same enthusiasm you reward success. We are *not* talking about the poor performer who consistently fails to meet expectations. We're talking about bright, committed individuals who happen to fail. Make it clear that the reward is not specifically for the failure, but rather, the concomitant learning that occurs as a result of this failure.

Box 6.3 provides a summary of this recovery approach.

PROACTIVE HINDSIGHT

To reduce the probability of the stifled communication error occurring, carefully assess your response to staff mistakes. Make sure you listen actively and don't overreact. Avoid chastising staff when things go wrong, recognizing that some of the biggest leaps in career development occur when mistakes become learning events. Become a coach who is skilled in debriefing problem situations.

BOX 6.3.

Summary of the Rebound Strategy
for Stifled Communication :
Rebound with Rapid Releasing

1. Immediately assess your response to staff mistakes.
2. Avoid blaming staff who did not fully communicate.
3. Diffuse anger.
4. Meet with your staff to acknowledge the problem and present your plan for change.
5. Develop a process for dealing with information that includes more checks and balances and rewards for those who reveal problem areas.

7

BUNGLED HIRING
Rebound with Rapid Revamping

WHAT THE MISTAKE LOOKS LIKE

Roberta C. is a midcareer leader in a fast-paced advertising firm employing approximately 300 staff members. The firm's owners are assertive leaders who tend to make decisions quickly, forming strong initial first impressions.

Roberta recently had an opening in the sales division that she leads and relied on the recommendation of the owners in hiring a new salesperson. The position was critical since the sales force is relatively small for the size of the company. The owners participated in interviewing three potential salespeople and had a "gut level" feeling that one of the candidates, Bill S., was ideal. Roberta had reservations and wanted to spend more time with the interviewing and assessment process, but she acquiesced to the owners. She was in a hurry to fill the position, had trouble finding candidates, and didn't want to make waves with the owners.

Bill S. turned out to be a highly ineffective salesperson. He was a bad fit for the culture of the organization, and his skills were way below the average for Roberta's existing sales force. Roberta had to fire him within three months, and her sales objectives were sorely compromised by the lost time. To make matters worse, the company lost two important accounts due to Bill's blunders.

Roberta realizes she made a big mistake in the way she handled the hiring process. She gave up too much control and did not utilize a process that would more reliably assess the best candidate for the job. She was too eager to avoid conflict and, subsequently, let down her sales force and damaged her credibility. Ironically, the owners did not take much responsibility for the problem and have placed the blame on Roberta.

THE CAUSES OF BUNGLED HIRING

While poor decision making, discussed in chapter 5 of this book, played a role in Roberta's hiring mistake, several additional elements come into play when talent is being sought by leaders. Hiring key people often entails receiving input from others who have a stake in the success of the unit into which new talent will be brought. Effective utilization of input under the pressure of scurrying to deal with a staff shortage provides an ideal context within which a leader might make the mistake we call *bungled hiring—failure to bring the right talent into the organization.* To be successful, leaders must have the courage to stand up for what they believe. Even if it results in conflict with senior leaders, leaders must be strong advocates for the type of talent they believe to be the best fit for their team. It's their team, after all.

Another cause of the talent acquisition problem is related to the often undetected differences between succession versus replacement planning. Replacement planning refers to replacing a staff person with a new hire based on the same job description as the old. This may be a very shortsighted approach because the skills needed to move an organization into the future may be dramatically different from those needed in the past. What worked in the past may have disastrous consequences in the future. Past successes do not guarantee that the same hiring practices will be effective in the future. Succession planning focuses on hiring to the needs of the organization—current and future—not simply finding an individual with relatively the same skill set to replace this person.

Not involving other key players in the equation may also cause the wrong hire. In our own consulting practices, we have discovered that this noninvolvement may cause the leader to make a hasty hiring decision. For example, how involved is the potential team of the candidate in the decision on whom to hire? We have seen a great many decisions head in the wrong direction, just because a team didn't have an opportunity to be a part of the interviewing and decision process. In particular, it's not just noninvolvement in the interview that's the culprit; it's also nonparticipation in the design of the interviewing process. We know from the research that involvement has a higher probability of being more effective than no involvement at all, from two vantage points:

- Higher quality decisions are typically made, and
- Better commitment to these decisions can result.

Still another cause is not being realistic about the position, where a leader can actually sell the position way too much. In some of the research on "realistic job previews," we know that there is a greater tendency to make an accurate decision when the candidate is given honest information about the position. The decision runs on both fronts—on the part of the candidate and the leader. So when leaders present just the glowing aspects of a position for the sake of good marketing and persuasion, there's a higher probability they're headed for trouble than if they present what the job really looks like.

A final cause of this error occurs when leaders have an "all-the-eggs-in-one-basket" hiring philosophy. They place all their stock in one primary candidate and become "sold" on that person early in the interview process. They then make unduly harsh judgments about subsequent candidates, comparing them to this one exalted "star." This is termed the halo effect. Of course, when a leader does this, the negative side of the star can be jaded to the positive.

The art of selecting the right person for a given position is difficult to master, and many leaders fall short in this area, making the critical mistake of bringing the wrong person into the fold. Lack of quick rebound action can result in being strapped with a weak player; this situation might take months, even years, to undue once legal conditions come into play.

REBOUND WITH RAPID REVAMPING

1. Review the new hire's weak performance with team members.

Find out who was involved in the hiring process. We're not talking about the human resources team, specifically, because they're the ones who likely provided guidelines and/or coaching for successful interviewing. Rather, we have found that when leaders do a retrospective consideration of who were the key players in this process, they have a better chance of recovering. If the leader involved a team in the process, then the entire team should be part of this step of the recovery. We're not suggesting any breach of confidentiality here by asking the team to make a firing decision. Rather, we are suggesting that the leader gather data from the team in terms of the performance of this new hire. Weigh this performance from two perspectives—what is expected and how the performance measures up here. When conducting this review, ask about whether the team has been conducting adequate coaching, just to be sure that all your bases are covered before moving to the next step. As part of this first phase, don't be clandestine here. Share with the individual that you'll be asking team members about how things are going. And do the same with the individual you have hired. Examine everyone in the same light.

2. Make sure to discern that it's a wrong hire and not poor performance management on your part.

This second phase is a critical one because you want to make sure you are not asking the person to leave prematurely. You need to have attempted methods such as coaching and performance management. There are many books and training programs out there on these methods, so we suggest that you consult them for more detailed information on best ways to conduct these strategies. Box 7.1 provides a quick reference on performance feedback for your review.

Box 7.1 is useful as an initial guide because it provides an opportunity for the individual to receive the best possible leadership from you and increases the probability that you are not just trying to railroad the individual out of the organization. In step 1 in box 7.1, you'll see that the leader needs to approach feedback constructively by not making any inferences or using sarcasm. Remember, you're here to help the individual and your organization. We also say to avoid absolutes. What we mean by this is telling the individual that "she always . . ." or "he never. . . ." This has a high probability of putting the individual on the defensive with responses such as "I don't always . . ." or "I remember an incident a few weeks ago where I did not do what you say I always do." What happens in these kinds

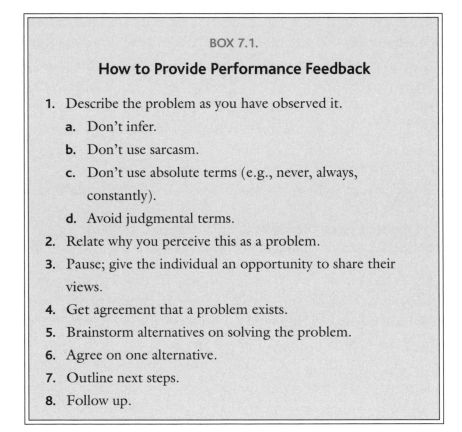

BOX 7.1.

How to Provide Performance Feedback

1. Describe the problem as you have observed it.
   a. Don't infer.
   b. Don't use sarcasm.
   c. Don't use absolute terms (e.g., never, always, constantly).
   d. Avoid judgmental terms.
2. Relate why you perceive this as a problem.
3. Pause; give the individual an opportunity to share their views.
4. Get agreement that a problem exists.
5. Brainstorm alternatives on solving the problem.
6. Agree on one alternative.
7. Outline next steps.
8. Follow up.

of situations is that the individual responds to the absolute word and debates this, rather than debating the behavior in question.

In step 2 in box 7.1, you need to relate why the individual's behavior or performance is an issue for you. Then, in step 3, pause. The purpose of this is to give the individual an opportunity to collect his or her thoughts and respond after reflecting on what you have said. In some circumstances, we have found that the individual may need a little time, so don't force the issue at this point. Feel free to have them come back the next day for their response. Then, in step 4, get agreement that a problem truly exists. If the individual says it does not, and in your estimation it does, then you'll need to let them know that while the individual may not agree with you, the problem is as you document it. Of course, in many organizations, the individual may have the opportunity to talk with someone in human resources or his or her union representative. If this is the case, encourage them to do so. Brainstorming of alternatives in step 5 provides an opportunity for both of you to engage in solution generation. And remember, involvement brings greater commitment. Make sure that neither of you critique prematurely; give yourself some time for adequate brainstorming. Agree on an alternative and a plan for follow-up.

Don't spend excess time in performance management feedback. If you are getting nowhere and your internal human resources consultants or external consultants are saying that you are doing all you can, you're ready to look at key behaviors that indicate to you even more clearly that you have hired the wrong person. Table 7.1 will help you discern direct cues that this was the wrong hire.

Many leaders simply need to spot the road signs that this may be an inappropriate hire, not a performance management issue. In the first scenario in table 7.1, where the person complains incessantly about the organization, for example, you'll hear that there are so many policies and procedures wrong in your organization. Another strong cue is that you may hear the individual complain that this is not the way things were in this person's previous organization. The leader may have tried to help the individual see the positives of the organization, but to no avail. The leader may have looked into the complaints and discovered that these are largely unfounded. Or the leader may have to say that this is the situation in the organization and the organization will not change—the individual needs to adjust.

If the individual continually voices concerns about many people in the organization, take note. The key word here is "many." If

TABLE 7.1.

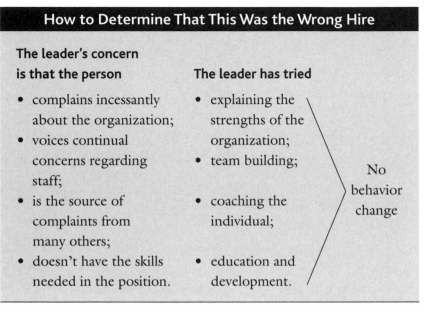

How to Determine That This Was the Wrong Hire	
The leader's concern is that the person	**The leader has tried**
• complains incessantly about the organization; • voices continual concerns regarding staff; • is the source of complaints from many others; • doesn't have the skills needed in the position.	• explaining the strengths of the organization; • team building; • coaching the individual; • education and development.

No behavior change

it's just one person, this may be an early warning sign and worth checking into, but it's not as serious as complaints about many. We have seen individuals complain not only about other staff and team members, but customers as well. And the complaints appear profuse and never ending. You may have tried some informal team building sessions with the internal staff having an issue, but this has not helped. Again, you probably made a wrong hire.

In the third example in table 7.1, you may find that many others are coming to you and stating how difficult it is to work with the new hire. The leader may have tried to address this concern with the individual; the individual responds with defensiveness and a refusal to make needed changes. You now know that performance feedback is probably not going to be of much use.

And in the final example of table 7.1, the individual may simply not have the skills or competencies to do the work. No amount of training or development is working to significantly change these skills or competencies. You've made a wrong hire. Period.

3. Have an honest conversation with top leaders who supported the hire.

Approach this meeting with facts, not emotions. Review the expected performance of the poor hire in contrast to the actual performance. Give specific examples. Then, after reviewing this information, either announce your decision to let the person go and what steps you are taking to terminate the employment relationship—or get the support for this action (if needed, of course). Then give your analysis of what went wrong in the hiring process, focusing on what you could have done differently by being firmer in your convictions and clearer about the type of talent needed. Delineate the actions you will take to develop a better talent selection process and more up-to-date hiring criteria.

Notice that in this step you are not addressing what you will do to coach the individual. You have already dealt with this through the human resources department or an external consultant. What you are doing is letting top leadership in on your immediate plan for action and engaging their support. Sometimes, leaders are reluctant to do this until it's way too late in the game. Then, it's a hard sell to let the new hire go. Clue the top leader(s) in on this early in the game. Elicit their support and suggestions.

This is precisely what Ken Fry told us he did with a wrong hire. Ken is the president of On the Scenes Production in Los Angeles. His situation involved a sales rep he had hired. For Ken, this third phase was critical because in talking with top leadership, they understood not only the problem but also the fact that "the interviewing process was not as in-depth as it should have been—the interviewing process was not a structured one. . . . sometimes you're in such a hurry to fill a position that you'll do anything." The fact that the interviewing process was a bit awry was a key catalyst here in helping the leadership team really look closely at this situation.

4. Take immediate action to remove the person who is a bad fit.

Assuming that you have already tried a number of strategies to rectify the poor performance, such as coaching and performance feedback, and these have failed, resist the temptation to try endless repeats of these to help the individual develop the skills needed. Just as important as it is for a leader to concentrate on what a leader does here, it's equally important for what a leader does not do. If there is no promise from the previous strategies, you'll need to move on to the immediate rebound. Continuing the coaching path is a no-win for both the leader and the poor hire. We're not saying that coaching won't work. What we have found is that, with the wrong hire, some leaders engage in too much coaching and not enough swift action. The individual is probably miserable, and so are you. While harsh, letting the individual go—with respect and dignity— may be a welcome relief to the wrong hire as well as the organization. Again, some coaching may certainly be warranted initially, but with the wrong hire, act swiftly.

Employing one strategy after another only adds fuel to the fire created by the hiring mistake in the first place. It's time to cut your losses and move on. Begin this step by consulting with your human resources department to determine what steps can be taken to remove the new hire from the position. If there is no human resources department in your organization, consult an external human resource consultant or attorney skillful in employment situations. If a probationary period was built into the employment contract, it may just be a matter of termination at the end of that period. If no probationary period was established, then careful documentation and evidence of poor performance may be needed. Don't make a legal blunder. Seek guidance if you're unsure.

5. If appropriate, help the individual find a better fit.

Remember, this is not specifically about poor performance, but a bad fit. Therefore, there may be other spots in your organization that may be appropriate for this individual. Or you may have colleagues in other organizations that could really profit from this individual's expertise. Think about this seriously. If you harbor resentment toward the individual, put this aside because it will get you nowhere pretty quickly. Your successful recovery will be based on a win-win situation. Part of this perspective may be letting the individual go and helping them find related work.

We have also found that even when you cannot find the individual related work, the fact that you have tried will provide positive momentum here. And trust us, you may need it! The individual will have a greater likelihood of perceiving you in a positive light—hence speeding up your own recovery.

One cautionary perspective: if, indeed, finding the individual alternative work is not appropriate, then you can move on. Notice that we did not state: skip this step! We're adamant that every leader in this circumstance needs to at least consider if it is appropriate for them to be a support in helping the individual find alternative employment. If not, then don't do it. But at least ask the question of yourself.

6. Establish a leadership team to review projected business needs and the type of talent that will be necessary to obtain the desired results.

This step requires strategic thinking on the part of key leaders in the organization. It is not just a future-oriented strategy, but a present-oriented one. Engaging in this step will have a greater probability of restoring the support of top leadership and your team than if you omit it. You're now geared to the present mistake by focusing on the future. If a strategic plan has been developed for the organization, begin with a review of this document. Then determine the competencies needed for new hires in order to implement the strategic plan with successful outcomes. Think carefully about skills that were relevant in the past, but will be less useful in moving the organization into the future. For example, establishing immediate rapport and quick face-to-face relationship building might have been critical for salespeople in the past. However, if your organization is utilizing more online, virtual contact with potential customers, the ability to establish relationships without face-to-face contact may be more critical.

Also reflect on the area(s) that strategic planning experts call "emergents." These are variables that need to be considered because, while they are not critical now, they will be in the future. Here an organization's strategic plan can provide some relevant cues. Look for key focus areas for future opportunities and see if they relate to your mis-hire. If so and based on your conversation with top leaders, determine what you would do differently in the future and explain how you would use these emergents as part of the hiring process. As you can see, here you're focusing on the future but also using this to plan immediately, thus restoring people's confidence in you. This is precisely what Ken Fry, president of On-the-Scenes Productions, did. In Ken's words, "I went to the president and took a head-on approach and told him that we have to have a much more structured interviewing process, along with taking the time to check references. By putting in a better layer in the interviewing process—built on checks and balances—you'll have greater assurances that you're bringing in the right person. The 'aha' for me was that you can bring in some noncore individuals on a contract basis and keep looking for the right individual. Sometimes we just work a little too quickly."

7. Let others know about your mis-hire, as appropriate.

Look also beyond the strategic plan to your own behaviors. What did you do that may have been a catalyst in the mis-hire? What was your part in prolonging the individual's mis-hire? What you should not do, once the individual has been let go, is bad-mouth the person. This will take away from all the good work you have done to this point. Even if blaming is justified, it rarely works in your favor. Remember, it's a mis-hire, not a bona fide performance problem. Some leaders have asked us about whether they should say something in dire circumstances (e.g., the mis-hire lied on her application, and this lie was crucial to their successful performance). We believe justice is never well served by relating this to others. Better to simply state that you have made a decision to let the individual go. Period. Remember: this is your recovery.

Box 7.2 provides a summary of the recovery strategies for bungled hiring.

PROACTIVE HINDSIGHT

To avoid this type of mistake, refer to step 6 of the recovery strategy. Make sure the competencies needed for the new position are aligned with the strategic plan of the organization. This requires continual updating of performance requirements to ensure new talent is a good fit. Stringent assessing of candidates for staff positions will also decrease the probability that you'll make a bad hire.

BOX 7.2.

Summary of the Rebound Strategy for Bungled Hiring: Rebound with Rapid Revamping

1. Review the new hire's weak performance with team members.
2. Make sure to discern that it's a wrong hire and not poor performance management on your part.
3. Have an honest conversation with top leaders who supported the hire.
4. Take immediate action to remove the person who is a bad fit.
5. If appropriate, help the individual find a better fit.
6. Establish a leadership team to review projected business needs and the type of talent that will be necessary to obtain the desired results.
7. Let others know about your mis-hire, as appropriate.

CHAPTER 8

FATAL ERRORS
Failures that Rarely
Result in a Comeback

Are all mistakes recoverable through rapid rebound strategies? Absolutely not, according to our research. The rapid rebound strategies we have identified previously in this book will not work when two specific types of fatal errors are committed:

1. Aberrations of trust that compromise leader integrity, and
2. A pattern of foolish mistakes that indicates gross incompetence.

Beware! Leaders who have engaged in the fatal errors we are about to describe have permanently derailed their careers.

FATAL ERROR TYPE 1: ABERRATIONS OF TRUST THAT COMPROMISE LEADER INTEGRITY

Gross dishonesty, embezzling, and covering up critical information stockholders must have are characteristic of this type of fatal error. Why would a leader risk being caught in such high-risk behavior? One school of thought, says Mark Ingebretsen in *Why Companies Fail* (2003), suggests that people engage in illegal behavior in organizations because it's easy to get away with it! Simply put, it's hard to catch and prosecute corporate criminals. Juries typically get bogged down in the details surrounding corporate crime, and prosecutors therefore have difficulty proving the deed occurred beyond a reasonable doubt. Internal controls are often poor or not effectively monitored. So it is tempting and relatively easy to alter the numbers or actually steal. And the stock market rewards falsified numbers until, of course, they are discovered. The decade of the '90s may be remembered as one characterized by "high fliers." Aggressive CEOs like Enron's Kenneth Lay, Tyco's Dennis Kozlowski, and WorldCom's Bernard Ebbers mesmerized the public by their willingness to break the rules. As scandal after scandal occurred, however, the public's fascination with these failed leaders waned. High-flying risk takers often find themselves spending a great deal of time and energy covering their tracks, losing sight of the organizational big picture.

Greed is often a prime motivator of high fliers as they strive for more power and conquests, often addicted to the danger and excitement taking risks provides. When the economy is strong, some leaders are more tempted to take unwarranted risks. Research has demonstrated that the very skills needed to reach the top of most organizations enhance a tendency toward risk taking and innovation. Putting aside the dangers, leaders may, under the pressures to "make the numbers" and please stockholders or compete successfully in the marketplace, be tempted to stretch the truth. "Aberrations of trust and compromises of integrity, e.g., theft, these are career killers," says one of our interviewed leadership coaches, David Bachrach, president of the Physician Executive's Coach. In his interview with us he drew a parallel with academic medicine: "There is no tolerance for this in academic medicine. One does not lie or steal. One does not cook research data. One does not injure patients by incompetence or inattention." Likewise, you don't do this in leadership either. And if you do, there is an extremely high probability your career will be derailed or irreparably damaged.

In *Why Smart Executives Fail* (2003), Sydney Finkelstein states that the single most important indicator of potential executive failure is lack of character. Finkelstein defines character as having high ethical standards, deep competence, and a desire to help others succeed; acknowledging when something is wrong; and promoting honesty. Roderick Kramer's research (2003) on reckless leadership juxtaposes success with the consequences of forgoing integrity. Those who stay on the righteous path say their personal character and core values buffer them from the temptation to let personal power go amok. They are prudent in their behavior, sending up trial balloons before moving full steam ahead into risky ventures. They worry about the routine operations and details of the business, making sure they are fully informed. And they take time to reflect on their actions and behavior. This approach stops them from making the fatal error of going down the path failed leaders walk—from stretching the rules to unethical behavior to even criminal acts.

In our interview with leadership coach Dr. Steve Lundin, coauthor of the multimillion-copy, best-selling book *Fish!* (2000), we learned about the relationship between a leader's core (a stable and deeply held set of values and beliefs that have been tested in the fires of life) and the probability of derailment. The metaphor that Steve uses to define this core is an "internal values mirror"—one that the leader uses to "reflect on judgments, consider appropriate responses to fierce situations, and determine when to make a personal commitment." Steve suggests that without such a core, tested and hardened by the fires of life, we are prone to make decisions that breach trust and violate integrity. Without a core we will not have the consistency in our actions and our treatment of others that constitutes character. He sums up this perspective on how difficult it is to recover from a pattern of decision making without the consistency provided by a core with a quote he attributes to Stephen Covey: " 'You can't talk your way out of the problem you behaved your way into.' " Our research clearly validates this viewpoint. If you look at the leaders who have committed fatal errors while heading up Enron, Tyco, WorldCom, and others, you'll see that these leaders were not always reckless with their careers. They had outstanding track records—both productively and ethically. But they got in trouble when they went against their "core" and committed some unethical practices. The probability is quite low that a leader will recover from these. And if recovery occurs, it will likely be after a significant period of time or in a career quite different from the one in which the leader was successful.

FATAL ERROR TYPE 2: A PATTERN OF FOOLISH MISTAKES THAT INDICATES GROSS INCOMPETENCE

Sometimes leaders fail and cannot recover because their deeds are simply unintelligent responses to certain situations. Warning signs include inability to recall important facts, jumping to indefensible conclusions, and not being able to deal with complex, ambiguous situations. This may result in a single-minded, obstinate, uninformed approach to decision making that leads to disaster. Does this mean a leader has to be a mental giant to succeed? Not entirely. In fact, being brilliant can be intimidating to others and has been shown to cause some leaders to dismiss the ideas of others. Yet, an ability to communicate is correlated with leadership success.

The bottom line with fatal error type 2 is that there needs to be a pattern of unintelligent responses. No one is perfect and from the research on perfectionism (see chapter 1), we know that most of us can learn from our mistakes and alter our patterns. However, in the type 2 fatal error, leaders continue making these mistakes, demonstrating a lack of intellectual capacity to learn and self-correct.

Foolish errors can result from a seemingly nonexistent aptitude to develop leadership skills. Daniel Goleman's research on Emotional Intelligence (EI), for example, suggests that effective leaders have the capacity to build relationships throughout their organization. Those who seem unable to develop EI are unable to communicate, listen, and "connect" with the very people they are attempting to lead. Their interpersonal bunglings look clumsy and immature, damaging their capacity to get the cooperation they need to execute what needs to get done. One of our interviewees, Dr. Jacqueline Byrd, described the extreme interpersonal deficit of treating others as if they are worthless, calling them "stupid" and other names. While arrogance may be a recoverable flaw, when a behavior goes to this extreme it demonstrates a total absence of EI and, says Byrd, "It cannot be recovered from." Aptitude deficits might also appear in a leader's inability to master budgeting, goal setting, business writing, presentation skills, interviewing—any of the core competencies needed for effectiveness.

Another example is not understanding the core business within which you are leading. Dr. Val Arnold is senior vice president, Executive Services and a leadership coach at Personnel Decisions

International (PDI, Inc.). In our interview, Dr. Arnold said, "I have observed leaders capable of sufficiently mastering one level of leadership within their organizations, but who cannot master the next level to which they are promoted and, consequently, are inept at running their business and achieving expected business outcomes. Often, basic errors in fundamental practices or incomplete mastery of broader business savvy become associated with the leader on the road to demise." Foolish errors deem leaders who make them incompetent, fatally wounding their credibility with others at every level in the organization. Once labeled as inept, a leader cannot gain ground again and must recognize that leadership roles are not a good personal fit. Richard Chant, an outplacement expert with Wellington Search who works with leaders, says, "You cannot recover from a very poor job fit. Motivated abilities are key here."

CHAPTER

9

STRATEGIC
RAPID REBOUND

From Rebound Anxiety
to Rebound Competency

REBOUNDING WITH CONFIDENCE

Now that you have a detailed view of each recovery strategy and the fatal errors from which recovery is almost impossible, you are prepared to confront each mistake that you make with confidence that you can land on your feet. Don't forget a key premise of this book. Successful leaders do make mistakes. In fact mistake making is often necessary to develop the skills and character to become strong in the leadership role. Making mistakes can enhance your career rather than destroy it, if you know how to skillfully recover. So don't panic when you inevitably make a mistake. With our book by your side, move at once to develop an effective rapid rebound strategy.

We've created a summary of each of the seven mistakes and the accompanying rapid rebound strategies to jolt your memory as a ready reference guide (table 9.1). Determine which category your mistake falls into, then apply the strategies described. Of course, you may find your mistake is not a perfect fit and will require using strategies delineated in more than one category.

MOVING FROM REBOUND ANXIETY TO REBOUND ORIENTATION

We have found that with the seven rebound strategies there's a tendency for rebound anxiety. Here, leaders can become overwhelmed by where to begin because they can see bits and pieces of themselves in several of the mistakes. This overwhelming feeling is what we refer to as rebound anxiety. To prevent this, we have found particular success with *The Dance of Change* (Senge et al. 1999, 11). This is illustrated in table 9.2.

Applying the matrix from table 9.2, a leader who has made more than one critical mistake will take immediate action in quadrant 1—focusing on those mistakes that are of the highest impact and easiest to solve. Here, a leader would first review table 9.1 and then determine the one mistake that, if successfully rebounded, would create the highest impact for the leader personally or organizationally *and* take the least effort to accomplish. In consulting with leaders, we have learned that once they address the mistake(s) in quadrant 1, they can then move to quadrant 2. Effective leaders focus more on these two quadrants than on quadrants 3 and 4. Doing this, leaders can quickly move from rebound anxiety to rebound competency.

STRATEGIC REBOUND SKILLS

In our interview research of successful leaders, we have discovered that there are rebound perspectives that can expedite a leader's

TABLE 9.1.

Rapid Rebound Matrix

Mistake Type	Causes	Rebound Strategies
1. Engagement Gridlock: Failure to Use Staff	• Perfectionism to a fault. • Lack of understanding of your staff's needs. • Unwillingness to delegate interesting or important work. • Noninclusion of staff in critical decision making or problem solving. • Not developing staff talent. • Not letting staff know how decisions will be made.	Rebound with Rapid Reinvesting 1 Immediately clear your calendar. 2 Listen intensely, separating your feelings from the facts. 3 Fight hard to regain staff confidence by responding to feedback, then immediately acting.
2. Misaligned Momentum: Failure to Align Goals with Strategic Initiatives	• Overly enamored with a project not aligned with organizational strategy. • Independent and strong-willed personality type. • Loss of organizational direction in one's area.	Rebound with Rapid Redirecting 1 Recognize and admit you are heading in the wrong direction. 2 Present facts about what's not working and why. 3 Protect staff from penalties.

(Continued)

TABLE 9.1.

Continued

Mistake Type	Causes	Rebound Strategies
3. Political Misread: Failure to Accurately Assess Political Dynamics	• Not attuned to the power of political relationship building. • Too focused on own work unit.	Rebound with Rapid Repositioning 1 Analyze the political landscape. 2 Profile key individuals. 3 Build your alliance. 4 Rebuild relationships. 5 Look to a future project. 6 Give away the credit.
4. Too Much, Too Soon: Failure to Assess Readiness Level for a Given Assignment	• Enamored by the offer to assume a leadership role. • Lack of leadership development. • Overestimating one's own abilities. • Lack of emotional maturity.	Rebound with Rapid Reinventing 1 Decrease interactions with those you've alienated. 2 Seek advice on position success factors. 3 Use 360-degree feedback to gain perspective and choose a mentor. 4 Within thirty days, increase visibility with new approach.

(Continued)

Mistake Type	Causes	Rebound Strategies
5. Miscued Decision Making: Failure to Effectively Utilize Information or the Right Process to Make a Sound Decision	• Poor or incomplete information. • Inadequate decision-making process. • Relevant information is overlooked.	Rebound with Rapid Redesigning 1. Acknowledge and take full responsibility. 2. Assemble a SWAT team to problem solve. 3. Analyze what went wrong. 4. Make sure you know what information you need. 5. Apologize.
6. Stifled Communication: Failure to Create a Work Environment Where Staff Openly Communicate	• Instilling fear by being punitive. • Establishing psychological distance to avoid close interactions. • Judgmental questioning.	Rebound with Rapid Releasing 1 Immediately assess your response style to staff mistakes. 2 Avoid blaming staff who do not fully communicate. 3 Diffuse anger. 4 Meet with your staff to acknowledge the problem and present your plan for change. 5 Develop a process that includes more checks and balances and rewards for those who reveal problem areas.

(Continued)

TABLE 9.1.

Continued

Mistake Type	Causes	Rebound Strategies
7. Bungled Hiring: Failure to Bring the Right Talent into the Organization	• Moving too quickly. • Using stale hiring criteria. • Not involving the right people. • Overselling the organization to job candidates. • Being biased with an overly positive view of one candidate.	Rebound with Rapid Revamping 1 Revisit the new hire's performance with the hiring team. 2 Discern the difference between a wrong hire and poor performance management. 3 Have an honest conversation with top leaders who supported the hire. 4. Remove the bad hire. 5. If appropriate, help the individual find a better fit. 6 Establish a leadership team to review projected business needs and talent necessary. 7. Let others know of your mis-hire.

TABLE 9.2.

Where to Begin Immediate Rebound Action		
	Easy to Accomplish	Difficult to Accomplish
High Impact	1	2
Low Impact	3	4

rebound capacity. To enact the rapid rebound strategies summarized above, leaders will have greater success if they have the mind-set to rebound in the most expedient way. The following Rapid Rebound Skill Survey (box 9.1) will help you determine if you are prepared to rebound quickly. If you find you are lacking any of the skills delineated on the survey, your rebounding capacity will be bogged down and you may not be able to recover as fully as you would like. Understanding your areas of improvement here will position you to be as ready as possible for speedy action, when the time arises.

Continue to develop your rapid rebounding capability. Be on the lookout for other leaders in your organization who make mistakes and are able to get back up on their feet with minimal disruption to your organization. Watch them carefully, observing what skills they use. If possible, talk with them to debrief the mistake you observed and find out more about how they approached their recovery.

Remember this: The ability to recover from mistakes is the newfound leadership competency. When you master it, you will likely be more successful within the complex environment in which organizations operate. There is no doubt that you will make mistakes. How you recover will make you stand out from the leadership pack and increase your effectiveness, both personally and organizationally.

So go out and find your way through the muck of leadership mistakes. Pinpoint your priority mistake needing action. Focus on

BOX 9.1.

Rapid Rebound Skill Survey

Directions

Indicate the degree with which you agree or disagree with the following statements by using the following scale:

Strongly Disagree	Disagree	Agree	Strongly Agree
1	2	3	4

Respond by circling the number corresponding to the degree to which you engage in the following behaviors:

1. Being self-critical in analyzing my role in the creation of a problem.   1 2 3 4

2. Facilitating a group of people to assist me with problem solving.   1 2 3 4

3. Finding a mentor who can advise me on a given leadership issue.   1 2 3 4

4. Giving an effective apology.   1 2 3 4

5. Setting up a process to receive feedback from others with whom I work.   1 2 3 4

6. Responding nondefensively to feedback.   1 2 3 4

7. Determining which organizational information is most important.   1 2 3 4

8. Building productive relationships in my organization.   1 2 3 4

9. Presenting information in a logical manner.   1 2 3 4

10. Presenting information in a persuasive manner.   1 2 3 4

11. Working with a human resources consultant to fire a staff person.   1 2 3 4

12. Setting up a process to abruptly halt a project in progress.   1 2 3 4

13. Abruptly stopping one initiative and beginning another.   1 2 3 4

14. Identifying my leadership weaknesses.   1 2 3 4

15. Capitalizing on my leadership strengths.   1 2 3 4

16. Surrounding myself with other staff who compensate for what I don't do well.   1 2 3 4

17. Responding in a nonthreatening way to staff mistakes.   1 2 3 4

18. Establishing a process for checks and balances within my work unit.   1 2 3 4

19. Utilizing a structured problem-solving process.   1 2 3 4

20. Soliciting input from a variety of people in order to solve a problem.   1 2 3 4

Directions for Scoring

Add up the 4s, 3s, 2s, and 1s you have circled, giving each its absolute value.

60+   You are in excellent shape to begin rapid rebounding.

40–59   You are not quite ready to rebound rapidly, but a review of strategies will provide ability and motivation.

20–39   Begin intense study of all rapid rebound strategies to build your skills and confidence.

building capacity for future mistakes. Kevin Cashman, CEO of LeaderSource and author of several best-selling leadership books, said in his interview with us, "We see four key things that leaders need to do:

1. Admit to yourself that there was something you didn't know that you needed to know (openness).
2. Admit to others there's something missing.
3. Over time build self-awareness and self-reflection as a practice.
4. Learn some new behaviors that embody what was missing before.

Life is about recovery and learning. The most successful leaders I see are the most resilient people—it's not the survival of the fittest but the survival of the most resilient. It's a requirement of living, not just leadership."

We hope you have discovered how to become a more successful leader through rapid rebound. If you want to be better at something, it's not enough to just read or talk about it. You must act. We have given you the road map. But the most important marker is you. Commit to change. Do it. Share the learning with others.

REFERENCES

Allen, B. 2002. "Sorry About That." *StarTribune*, December 21, B5.

Argyris, C. 2000. *Flawed Advice and the Management Trap*. Oxford: Oxford University Press.

Beith, M. 2002. "Transition." *Time*, July 1, 10.

Bennis, W. 1989. *The Leader Within*. Irvine, CA: LearnCom, Inc.

Bennis, W., and Nanus, B. 1997. *Leaders: Strategies for Taking Charge*. Scranton, PA: HarperBusiness.

Blatt, S. J. 1995. "The Destructiveness of Perfectionism." *American Psychologist* 50, no. 12 (December): 1003–20.

Brown, W. S. 1985. *13 Fatal Errors Managers Make and How You Can Avoid Them*. East Rutherford, NJ: Berkley Publishing Group.

"The BusinessWeek Fifty." *BusinessWeek*, 105.

Charan, R., and Colvin, G. 1999. "Why CEOs Fail." *Fortune*, June 21, 69–78.

Cone, J. 1998. Online communication in entreworld.com. EntreWorld Web Resource, July 6. Kansas City, MO: Kauffman Center for Entrepreneurial Leadership at the Ewing Marion Kauffman Foundation.

"Dot Gone." 2000. *Wired*, August, B4.

Dotlich, L. and Cairo, C. 2003. *Why CEOs Fail*. San Francisco: Jossey-Bass.

Duck, J. 2001. *The Change Monster: The Human Forces that Fuel or Foil Corporate Transformation and Change*. New York: Crown Business.

Edmondson, A., Leonard, D., and Cannon, M. 2000. *Harvard Management Update* 5, no. 4 (April): 8.

Essex, L., and Kusy, M. 1999. *Fast Forward Leadership*. London: Financial Times-Prentice Hall.

Farkas, C. M., and Wetlaufer, S. 1996. *Maximum Leadership: The World's CEOs Share Their Five Strategies for Success*. New York: Henry Holt.

Finkelstein, S. 2003. *Why Smart Executives Fail*. New York: Portfolio.

Funderburg, L. 2001. "The F Word." *O Magazine*, September, 275–79.

Gaines-Ross, L. 2003. "It's (Not That) Hard to Say You're Sorry." *Chief Executive* 188 (May).

Goldsmith, M. 2003. "Adding Value, but At What Cost?" *Fast Company* 73 (August): 58.

Goleman, D. 1995. *Emotional Intelligence*. New York: Bantam.

———. 1998. "What Makes a Leader?" *Harvard Business Review* 76, no. 6 (November–December): 82-91.

———. 2003. "Leadership That Gets Results." *Harvard Business Review* (March–April): 77–90.

Goodwin, D. K. 1998. "Lessons of Presidential Leadership." *Leader to Leader*, Summer, 23–27.

Hammonds, K. 2000. "How Do We Break Out of the Box We're Stuck In?" *Fast Company* 40 (November): 260–68.

Healey, J. R. 2001. "What's Ahead for Ford? Lots of Turmoil." *USA Today*, December 6.

"Hiring Someone Who Has Failed: Sensible or Foolish Choice?" 2000. *Leadership Strategies* 3, no. 7 (July): 8.

Ingebretsen, M. 2003. *Why Companies Fail*. New York: Crown Business.

Kirsner, S. 1998. "The Best Defense: Part I." *Fast Company* 16 (August): 142.

Kotter, J. 1988. *The Leadership Factor*. New York: MacMillan Inc.

Krackhardt, D., and Hanson, J. 1993. "Informal Networks: The Company Behind the Chart." *Harvard Business Review* 71, no. 4 (July): 104–11.

Kramer, R. N. 2003. "The Harder They Fall." *Harvard Business Review* 81, no. 10 (October): 58–66.

Labich, K., and de Llosa, P. 1994. "Why Companies Fail." *Fortune*, November 14, 52-58.

Lombardo, M. M., and Eichinger, R. W. 1992. *Preventing Derailment: What to Do before It's Too Late*. Greensboro, NC: Center For Creative Leadership.

Lundin, S. C., Paul, H. and Christensen, J. 2000. *Fish! A Remarkable Way to Boost Morale and Improve Results*. New York: Hyperion.

Magnier, M. 2000. "An Economic Tsunami." *StarTribune*, October 6, D1, D5.

Martin, M. 2004. "2004 Platinum Honor Roll: 25 Best Managed Companies in America." *Forbes*, January 7.

Maxwell, J. 2000. *Failing Forward*. Nashville: Thomas Nelson Publishers.

McCall, M. 1998. *High Flyers*. Boston: Harvard Business School Press.

McCall, M., and Lombardo, M. 1983. *Off the Track: How and Why Successful Executives Get Derailed*. Technical Report No. 21. Greensboro, N.C.: Center for Creative Leadership.

McDermott, L. 2001. "Developing the New Young Managers." *Training and Development*, October, 43.

Norcross, J. C., Ratzin, A. C., and Payne, D. 1989. "Ringing in the New Year: The Change Processes and Reported Outcomes of Resolutions." *Addictive Behaviors* 14: 205–12.

Nutt, P. 1999. "Surprising but True: Half the Decisions in Organizations Fail." *Academy of Management Executive* 13, no. 4:75.

Pham, A. 2000. "Failure Has Found Status among Net Companies." *StarTribune*, October 30, D1, D9.

Polivy, J., and Herman, C. P. 1999. "The Effects of Resolving to Diet on Restrained and Unrestrained Eaters: The 'False Hope Syndrome.'" *International Journal of Eating Disorders* 26: 434–47.

———. 2000. "The False Hope Syndrome: Unfulfilled Expectations of Self-Change." *Current Directions in Psychological Science* 9: 28–131.

Robbins, H., and Finley, M. 1995. *Why Teams Don't Work: What Went Wrong and How to Make It Right*. Princeton, NJ: Peterson's Guides.

Sellers, P. 1995. "So You Fail . . . Now Bounce Back!" *Fortune*, May 1, 48–65.

Senge, P., Kleiner, A., Roberts, C., Ross, R., Roth, G., and Smith, B. 1999. *The Dance of Change*. New York: Currency Doubleday.

Smith, D. 1999. *Make Success Measurable! A Mindbook-Workbook for Setting Goals and Taking Action*. New York: John Wiley & Sons.

Stoltz, P. 2004. "Building Resilience for Uncertain Times." *Leader to Leader* 18 (Winter), 16–20

Terhune, C., McKay, B., and Lublin, J. S. 2004. "At Coke, Heyer's Style is a Concern." *Wall Street Journal*, February 23, A4.

"The Top 25 Managers." 2001. *BusinessWeek*, January 8, 62–78.

Voh Drehle, D. 1993. "The Crumbling of a Pillar in Washington." *Washington Post*, August 15, A20–A21.

Waldroop, J., and Butler, T. 2000. "Managing Away Bad Habits." *Harvard Business Review* 78, no. 5 (September–October): 89–98.

What about Bob? Touchstone Video, August 20, 1996.

Wood, A., and Tracy, B. 2000. *The Traits of Champions: The Secrets to Championship Performance in Business, Golf, and Life*. Provo, UT: Executive Publishing.

INDEX